To my children, Hannah, Jessica and George
of whom I am inordinately proud,
thank you for your unfailing support of
everything I put my mind to.

PRAISE

'Lucy has a wonderful way of presenting information and ensuring you understand each and every concept.'

JO MILES, Exella

'I found Lucy Matthews' book a real eye opener into the world of PR. Lucy certainly knows her stuff and I can recommend her to anyone who wants to get serious about making their business stand out from the crowd.'

BARRY ALLAWAY, Ninja Business Tools

'I had never really been clear on the difference between PR and marketing but Lucy makes it very easy to understand with lots of hints and tips on how we can use it to our advantage to promote our businesses.'

LIZ SPROTSON, Lawyers on Demand

'Lucy Matthews clearly knows her stuff and imparts it in an easy to digest way.'

LORRAINE ASHOVER,
Minerva Procurement Consultancy Services

'Great advice, professionally presented with lots of great PR tips to action.'

KERRIE ELLIS, The Image Advantage

'Lucy makes what seems impossible very do-able.'

LIZ SCOTT, The Image Advantage

'Lucy demystifies the world of PR, making it clear that anyone can have a go and it need not cost a fortune!'

SUZANNE MITCHELL, Swale Dale
Country Holidays

'The Dark mysteries of PR are no longer dark. There are loads of books written about PR that confuse and terrify the novice. This book is filled with simple steps that just make so much sense. Great for beginners and experienced PR people. I am never too old to learn! Worth its weight in gold!'

ADRIAN BROWN, 2be2Serve

'Written in an engaging and accessible way it sheds light on some of the PR mysteries and enables you to more cleverly work out ways to get the right sort of attention. A very useful resource.'

KARIN SLATER, Figura

'Lucy's book is marvellous! I embraced her teachings, years of knowledge-honing skills, which made getting positive publicity so much easier and more effective than ever before.'

MARK EDWARDS, Getahead

CONTENTS

FOREWORD

When Lucy asked me to write the foreword to *A Marvellous Reputation* I was both flattered and perplexed in equal measure. Flattered that such an eminent Public Relations professional would call upon me, a plumber, to introduce her literary creation; but there was also the nagging question, demanding to know – why choose me?

The answer, it turns out, wasn't too hard to uncover and as I began to read Lucy's ideas it was clear that just below the surface of her personal story, which she clearly views as important to the formation of her approach to PR, exists the shadow of my own life journey and attitude to growing my business.

It's interesting just how different our backgrounds are: Lucy's 'rags to riches' story starts with the green knickers of her alma mater, Cheltenham Ladies' College; dabbles with a career on the stage; transitions through high pressure selling and ends up in Australia working for a major PR agency.

Mine, on the other hand, started on a south London council estate, incorporated a lot of bunking off from my local comp, a pipe dream of being a pro-boxer that ended in a hospital bed, and led to an apprenticeship in plumbing.

But somehow, Lucy and I have arrived at a very similar, and what I would call common sense, view of how PR is quite simply the best marketing tool any business,

large or small, can engage in to deliver results that far exceed any other form of marketing.

Woven into the fabric of the founding story of her Marvellous PR agency are Lucy's *10 lessons for entrepreneurs who want to be talked about*, which she outlines in ten short and punchy chapters. Each point is undoubtedly a valuable gem for all entrepreneurial types, but what shines through for me is Lucy's core belief, which I share, that everything that's worth doing in business can have its value enhanced by a PR strategy.

When I was on the tools as a self-employed plumber I realised early on that the money was in the big houses, and that the people who lived in such places had friends with equally impressive piles. They needed good tradesmen, but there weren't too many of my kind in their social circles. What I had to do was deliver a great job, but also make sure that I was noticed and recognised for what I had done, and the rest was down to word of mouth. That is to say, people talking about me!

Hopefully I was the polite but cheeky Cockney bloke who did a great job, didn't charge too much, and cleaned up afterwards. At least that was the message I wanted going out to all those in need of a plumber in Pimlico, Chelsea and London's other posh suburbs. Back then I was just a kid with some tools, who'd never heard of PR, but I knew how to win and keep business, and I've never looked back.

Throughout *A Marvellous Reputation* Lucy makes use of some great quotes to illustrate her points (another thing she has in common with me). She opens with the Oscar Wilde classic: 'There is only one thing in the world worse than being talked about, and that is not being talked about.' And while it's definitely a PR industry staple, I think the sentiment in, 'Next to doing the right thing the most important thing is to let people know you are doing the right thing' captures PR for me. That genius came from industrialist and philanthropist, John D. Rockefeller.

There is of course a catch, and Lucy nails it and names it early – the Paradox of PR. Which is that the very people who need to harness the power of PR most, the small businesses, the start-ups, those working their guts out for a better future from their kitchen tables, are the entrepreneurs, and also the business people, who least understand PR and what amazing differences it can make to their operations, and so don't consider it. Instead they consider PR to be the realm of the multi-national corporation, and so continue the cycle of failing to fully reap the benefits of their efforts.

Lucy has founded a career on rescuing, through education, those caught in the vortex of the Paradox of PR, and *A Marvellous Reputation* is a perfect life raft to salvation.

CHARLIE MULLINS OBE
Founder and Chairman of Pimlico Plumbers and
Author of *Bog Standard Business*
http://www.pimlicoplumbers.com

INTRODUCTION

> 'There is only one thing in the world worse than being talked about, and that is not being talked about.'
>
> *Oscar Wilde*

Public Relations (PR) is all about relationships. Creating and enhancing good relationships with everyone whose opinion of you could influence your dealings with others, and the skills behind developing, nurturing, and using them to further your success.

It follows that good PR skills are vital to your *personal* relationships as well as your business and commercial life. I truly believe that and have seen it work many, many times.

I know PR works and I am passionate about helping business owners large and small to understand its subtleties and power and use the skills I have learned through my career to influence other's opinions of themselves and their businesses, to hugely positive effect. I work with charities, the third sector, and even here PR is their number one marketing tool.

How do I know what I am talking about and why would you follow my advice? Because I know it works. I use the skills I will show you myself, every day, in every aspect of my life. They have turned my life around. And they will do the same for you too. Especially when you are in the company of your target audience which, as you will see later, includes everyone from your mum to your accountant, as well as obviously your customers and investors, all having an influence – because they have an opinion – on you, and your business, and how it is seen.

I have built up my own profile as a PR expert from having one small estate agent client, working on my own on the edge of the desk at home, sharing it with my family, to a six-figure income consultancy business, with backup staff, whilst still being a stay at home mum and then supporting myself and working pretty much part time. It is important to note that in building up the business, the biggest form of marketing I have used is PR. And at the various stages of my life, moving to different countries and needing to establish my family and myself and get settled, having a PR mind-set has really helped.

I am using it all the time. I know what message I want to get across to whomever I am meeting and I try and make sure I behave in the way that makes that person feel comfortable, whilst remaining authentic to myself

and subtly getting my message over. I am always aiming for our meetings to be smooth and memorable. People with obvious chips on their shoulders and inferiority complexes and issues are not easy to be around. Using the skills highlighted by Dale Carnegie in his famous self-development book *How to Win Friends and Influence People*, I am constantly looking to make more connections, and to build their positive opinion of me, so that they will help me achieve the success I am seeking. Be it in my business or my personal life.

I know it is working when I hear someone say, 'I see your name everywhere, Lucy. You are obviously doing really well.' Or, 'I gather you are really busy – or at least that's how you appear – business must be good, we must talk soon about you working for me.' Excellent. Other people are boasting for me, and my reputation is winning me new business without me having to say anything.

And in my personal life: 'You seem to have so many friends and such a busy life! Things must be good. I would love to meet for a drink soon and get to know you better!' Again, fantastic. Other people are saying I am fun to be with, my busy diary is suggesting I am popular (not always true!) and now people want a bit of that too. All without me having to blow my own trumpet!

A Marvellous Reputation is for entrepreneurs and business owners of companies of all sizes, who hate blowing their own trumpet but who know they are marvellous and the best at what they do. And who really want to show others that they are the person (or business) to be with – as a work colleague, boss, consultant, supplier, therapist, friend, lover, partner, whatever.

It is a collection of the important tactics and fundamentals of good PR, and shows how using them strategically whilst being authentic to yourself can seriously help your bottom line profits and your personal happiness. I have gathered this knowledge in my own career, and I want to share my own journey with you to illustrate how I learnt the essentials of PR. It is a journey which will take us from the revered architecture and character-forming education of Cheltenham Ladies College in Gloucestershire to the stages and sea sides of Exeter in Devon; to the buzz and warm beer of London; to the glistening harbour and vitality of Sydney, Australia; to the gentility and charm of leafy Surrey; to the multilingualism and fairy-tale castles of Luxembourg; and back to the peace and inspirational scenery of South Devon. Via large and small companies and every type of business.

A Marvellous Reputation is not meant to be a full explanation of all the PR skills and tools available to

us – and nor can it be. It is a fun reference book, an overview of the PR opportunities out there, providing the basic insights and tactics that you can then use to influence the opinions of those people who are important to you, and hence make your personal and work relationships richer, your business profiles higher, and the perceived value of your products and services astronomic. Who would not want that?

CHAPTER ONE

What Is Public Relations (PR)?

> 'To establish oneself in the world,
> one does all one can to seem
> established there already.'
>
> François De La Rochefoucauld

Although this is a book for all entrepreneurs and business owners, people starting up in business are the ones who most need PR but who, paradoxically, are also most unlikely to do it. They see it as costly, only for the big boys, and therefore not something they can afford to spend their precious time and money on at a time when both these commodities are at a premium.

This is so tragic. It is vital for such people to really understand and be using PR to create and build the Know, Like, and Trust element of all their relationships – with all their target audiences, particularly the media, so that warm customers find them and start working with them. As I know that young/new businesses often cannot afford to employ a PR consultant, *A Marvellous Reputation* will

show them how they can do a lot for themselves, at no cost, incorporating PR into their monthly work routines - and why it is so important that they do.

It is also valuable for those already running a company or who just need refreshing on what PR is all about, and how they might be able to use it better. There is a lot of noise about PR especially in relation to how it sits with social media, and it is really very simple.

People look to over-complicate PR, to make it sound like something only highly-experienced consultants can do for your business, but A Marvellous Reputation will show you how you can make it work for yourself; simply and cost-effectively.

So, what is PR – Public Relations?

According to the Chartered Institute of Public Relations:

'Every organisation, no matter how large or small, ultimately depends on its reputation for survival and success.

'Customers, suppliers, employees, investors, journalists and regulators can have a powerful impact. They all have an opinion about the organisations they come into contact with - whether good or bad, right or wrong. These perceptions will drive their decisions about

whether they want to work with, shop with and support these organisations.

'In today's competitive market, reputation can be a company's biggest asset – the thing that makes you stand out from the crowd and gives you a competitive edge. Effective PR can help manage reputation by communicating and building good relationships with all organisation stakeholders.'

And here is my definition of Public Relations:

'Public Relations is about reputation - the result of what you do, what you say and what others say about you.

'Public Relations is the discipline that looks after reputation, with the aim of earning understanding and support and influencing opinion and behaviour. It is the planned and sustained effort to establish and maintain goodwill and mutual understanding between an organisation and its public.'

Then there is third-party endorsement. Third-party endorsement is a highly effective way of telling the world how marvellous you are, without boasting. Others tell people that you are the perfect fit for them, not you. It therefore follows that the better your relationships

with those around you, who have an influence on the opinions of others, the more likely they are to talk favourably about you and the more effusive they will be in that endorsement.

I have seen in many of my own life and career experiences, that understanding and using the fundamental skills of PR in certain situations can make a real difference to my happiness.

This is supported by a conclusion from The Grant Study, part of the Study of Adult Development at Harvard Medical School into the source of happiness. It followed the lives of 268 men from youth to old age and showed that 'happiness is not down to the attributes that you are born with – it's more about emotional intelligence and skill at long-term relationships.'

If you are like most people, you shy away from those who are too pushy, arrogant and selling themselves. Even though you would quite like to be their friend – they do seem like fun – their exaggerated, in-your-face, brash manner just turns you off. And it is the same in your business world. Sometimes too much sales stuff, full of euphemisms and exaggerations, makes you cynical about what to believe and whom you can trust.

Now look in the mirror. How do you think you come over to people who meet you? Scary thought? It doesn't have to be if you make use of the PR skills I will show you, which are free and available to everyone. Though hugely under-used.

Before I go into this in detail, here's a little fun story which might help clarify in your mind exactly what PR is, in relation to other forms of marketing and how it can really transform your personal and work lives, in more ways than you'd think.

Phil walks into a party and sees a gorgeous girl. He goes up to her and says, 'Hey, I'm fantastic in bed.'

That is direct marketing.

He then turns to face all the partygoers and shouts, loudly: 'Hi everyone, my name's Phil and I am fantastic in bed! Come and meet me.'

That is advertising.

Phil then goes up to another gorgeous girl (this is a good party) and gets her telephone number. The next day he rings her up and says, 'Hi, remember me, I'm fantastic in bed.'

That is telemarketing. Stay with me, we are getting to the point of the story!

Now, one of these beautiful girls walks up to Phil at this (buzzing) party and asks, 'Aren't you the one who's fantastic in bed?'

That is brand recognition.

Then, Phil sees another lovely girl at the bar with another girl he has met before. He gets up and straightens his tie, walks up to them and buys them both a drink. The

girl he has known before introduces him to the one he fancies, and he carries on chatting to them, and complimenting them both. The one he fancies then says she is leaving, so he helps her off her bar stool, picks up her bag after she drops it, helps her on with her coat, opens the door for her, gets her a taxi home, gives her a gentle kiss on the cheek and waves her goodbye. He returns to the party and carries on looking after the other girl until she finds someone else she wants to talk to. The next day the girl he knew before rings up the one he fancies and says 'You know that guy you met last night, he is such a lovely man – and apparently fantastic in bed! Can I give him your number? You will have a great date with him.'

And that, fellow entrepreneurs and business owners, is public relations.

Get others to say it, and keep quiet

PR is all about influencing how people see you, in a gentle way, in order to make the person you are targeting really get to know you, feel comfortable with you and, eventually trust you, without feeling that you are directly selling to them. It is getting someone else to say, or suggest, how marvellous you are without you having to say anything.

Imagine if it's a journalist writing about what you do in a well-respected publication, or reporting it on radio or

television. What could be a bigger and better endorsement of you? Or a leading charity with whom you have worked, telling all its followers how generous and warm-hearted you are, and why they should work with you too. Again, you have not boasted – remaining quiet, demure and hugely attractive as a result.

You know this, of course. All the marketing gurus stress the value of testimonials (a version of third-party endorsement) in your marketing material, but think how valuable this can be if you extend it into every aspect of your life? What level of success would you achieve, if you can have people all around you commenting on what you are doing and how brilliantly you are doing it (in and out of the bedroom), what a great partner and friend you are, how being with you can really benefit other's lives, and how your business has been great for them, and they would so recommend you?

It is perfect for any of us who do not like to blow our own trumpet and tell people outright how perfect we are for them. We know we would be their best friend, we have so much in common; we understand we are so much kinder and more fun than their previous partner, they really should go out with us; and it is obvious our business would fit them perfectly. No, no. We can't say that. That is boasting and most unsavoury.

However, if someone else says it about us, in a nice roundabout way, we can hide behind it and maintain our

modesty. Job done. The PR paradox I see all the time, is that most people do not realise that they need to use PR even in their business world, let alone in their personal life.

Why is it so useful? Because it is all about the way you communicate to all your target audiences – from your family to your accountant, work colleagues, sports' team members, customers (past and present), suppliers, employees (past and present), and other influencers and investors, not to mention your relevant key journalists and competitors. It helps you manage all their opinions of you and your business – which could make or break you if they get misunderstood.

'I really like him – don't know much about him, but he seems like a nice bloke.'

We all have an opinion about the people and businesses with whom we come into contact. They may or may not be strong or rational opinions, but they will definitely have an effect on which people we decide to have a drink with, confide in, be close friends with, do business with, shop with or support in some way.

For example, if you have just moved into a new area and you go round and introduce yourself personally to your neighbours, take them a small gift, invite them round for a drink and rave about their wonderful neighbourhood, they will welcome you with open arms. Even better, if you

invite one of your ex-neighbourhood friends, from where you used to live, to the drinks, and they comment on what a very generous and kind neighbour you were to them, your new neighbours will feel they have struck gold. And you will have no problem getting someone to let the John Lewis deliveryman in, and if the alarm goes off unexpectedly at 3am, they won't complain.

You have to know, like and trust someone in order to do business with them – we all know and agree with that. PR is the tool that will help you win people over – in every aspect of your life. It will enable you to build and maintain a good reputation – and is your only resource when something bad happens to tarnish it.

Anyone starting up in business will really need to understand and use PR if they want to survive and succeed in the heady world of the small businesses owner – out of your comfort zone and with your head above the parapet and highly visible to everyone. Ultimately it is that image you have created so carefully, and what others are saying about you (equally carefully constructed), which will make your business stand out from your competitors.

Which leads me to another well-known adage:

'Keep your friends close and your enemies closer.'

Meaning, briefly, make sure that you are constantly protecting that chance of third-party endorsement

from those around you, by keeping their opinions of you positive. If you fall out with anyone, or feel that they may not be quite on side with you any more, think of subtle ways to win them back and keep a close eye on them and what they are saying in public, so that you can manage the message they give out about you. This is equally true of your love life.

Accidents and rumours can kill you

Research by Convergys Corp. found that one negative customer review on YouTube, Twitter, or Facebook could cost a company up to 30 customers. And negative rumours, a problem with one of your products or an internal crisis being played out in the press, will do exactly the same.

> 'A lie gets halfway around the world before the truth has a chance to get its pants on.'
> Winston Churchill

Knowing how to handle negative publicity can nip potentially catastrophic situations in the bud – or even enable you to turn them around completely. All it takes is for one thing to go wrong, and a lifetime of reputation building can be undone in just moments, especially now with social media making it easy for your customers to communicate with each other instantly, sharing good and bad news with the entire world with just a click. Crisis management (in plain English, a communications strategy to save your reputation) is

the PR tool for turning bad back to good in the reputation world, and it is what you need - because it works.

> 'I suspect in most companies the public relations person is down at No. 20 in the pecking order. But here, he is fighting incredibly important battles. If a negative story starts running away with itself in the press and is not dealt with fast, it can badly damage the brand, and so we put enormous weight on our PR people.'
>
> Sir Richard Branson

If you are spending time and energy building up (and marketing) your image, you would be mad not to have a crisis management strategy up your sleeve in case things go wrong. And the best people to help you are the media. You need to get out there now, find the journalists in your trade, local, regional papers and magazines who write regularly on your area of business, and that of your customers, and start communicating with them, influencing their opinion of you, positively – so that they will lift you out of the crowd and help if anything ever goes wrong.

It really is worth reflecting on, and managing the way you communicate; building and looking after good

relationships, with everyone including the media, all the time, who has an influence on your survival. You never know when you are going to need them and they can all make a big difference to your success.

PUBLIC RELATIONS LESSON

Dale Carnegie gives us the most brilliant set of tips and skills in his famous book *How to Win Friends and Influence People*, which you can, and should, be using all the time to strengthen your relationships with those people who have opinions of you – both personally and in relation to your business.

Here are five of his most important recommendations to help your communications strategies:

1 Always be polite, positive, never complain and compliment others honestly. Leave them wanting to know more about you.

2 To encourage people to like you ask them questions about themselves and listen carefully to their answers. Use their name as often as you can in conversation, and focus all your attention on them.

3 To win people over to your point of view, never enter into an argument, respect, and try your hardest to understand other people's take on things. Be honest and humble if you have got something wrong.

4 Always smile and be as friendly and interesting as you can.

5 To change people without giving offence or provoking resentment, give lots of praise, encouragement and recognition for what they have done and how they are getting better at it, and avoid giving orders and high-lighting their mistakes. Refer to your own mistakes first.

CHAPTER TWO

How It All Began - From Green Knickers To Hard Sell

> 'Character is like a tree and reputation like a shadow. The shadow is what we think of it; the tree is the real thing.'
>
> *Abraham Lincoln*

I went to Cheltenham Ladies' College from the ages of 11 to 18. Yes, thick green knickers, bibles on our heads to encourage good deportment, daily practice at sitting down in assembly without making any noise with our chairs, and remembering to cross our ankles not our legs – as it shows the world our aforesaid green knickers.

Fantastic school in the gorgeous Regency town of Cheltenham in Gloucestershire, founded in 1853 to pioneer girls' education with stunning, awe-inspiring buildings, matched by character-building teaching which gave me great exam results, confidence and optimism about my life and future career.

However, during my time there, there was never any mention of jobs in the world of marketing, and certainly

not PR. I did not discover that businesses marketed themselves in any other way than an advertisement until a few years into my working life.

My thing all through school was performing. Put me on a stage and I would come alive and I won lots of prizes at it. Ballet dancing, singing, acting, poetry reading, bible reading, even Latin reading (yes, I won a regional competition. I know) and all I wanted to do was go to drama school and take over from Felicity Kendall in *The Good Life*, and Cilla Black on *Blind Date*. Aspiring to be those ladies really shows my age.

My teachers and parents were not keen to let me audition straight away (I think they knew I would never make it so helped me avoid the heartache early), so they encouraged me to go to university first. Of course, I opted to study English and Drama, as it would mean acting my way through university – perfect, I thought. Little did I know.

I chose Exeter University in Devon because, quite simply, it seemed like such a lovely place; my brother had loads of friends who had been there and loved it; I wanted to be near the sea and Dartmoor; and, miraculously, it had English and Drama courses. I did no research whatsoever into the content of the course and it turned out to be not at all what I had anticipated.

Method acting

The course was experimental, non-conformist and very much method acting, which is described as:

> 'A technique of acting in which an actor aspires to complete emotional identification with a part, based on the system evolved by Stanislavsky and brought into prominence in the US in the 1930s. Method acting was developed by Elia Kazan and Lee Strasberg in particular, and is associated with actors such as Marlon Brando and Dustin Hoffman.'

Sadly, not what I was expecting. I found out well into my time there that they chose two private school people each year 'to rock the boat and cause friction which would be good for the group dynamic'. And I was one of them. Great, three years as a social experiment guinea pig.

The interview, during which I had to be a sausage, was very taxing. Yes, thank you, it was taxing – there were loads of people applying for very few places and it was only my sizzling in the pan movements that got me through. Well, and being from CLC I guess.

I really did not enjoy my time on the drama element of the course (loved the English and social side of university life) and ended up with very low self-esteem and feeling I was never going to make it as an actress, or a performer of any kind. I needed to find a different career.

After flirting with accountancy (a very brief affair), I ended up selling display-advertising space, over the phone, for *Campaign*, the magazine for the advertising industry.

We had rigorous training and had to learn a very clever technique and follow it closely to get people to part with their cash, over the phone, and buy a blank space in a magazine, every month. I quickly realised that my drama skills were really helping me pretend, to my prospects, that I was a hotshot salesperson, really great at my job and loved what I was doing when in fact I was hating it and finding it really hard to do.

I also found that my innate curiosity and genuine interest in people got me easily through the first few parts of the hard sell. I would introduce myself and the proposition, find out enough about them and their business needs to move them on to the stage in the sales-patter, where I would ask: 'so if I could show you something that would give you all those things that you are looking for now for your business, would you be interested in hearing more?' At which point they were supposed to say, 'Yes, yes.' I was supposed to then rattle through the unique selling points of the deal and bang, the sale was supposed to be made.

However, for me it never happened. I just used to clam up. I absolutely could not close the sale no matter how hard I tried to use the phrases and arguments I had

been taught, and I would end up just giving them information about the magazine and agreeing to leave it with them to call me back if they wanted to buy. Which of course they rarely did.

What I was actually doing, although I didn't realise it, was PR for the magazine – not selling.

I was really struggling to achieve my targets. Then, fate struck. I am a fatalist. I believe we make our own luck by being aware of everything going on around us, and allowing fate to move us in the right direction. More on that later.

One month the magazine did a special feature on PR and we had to sell space around it to PR consultancies. I read the feature over and over, rang a load of prospects to sell them space in the normal way, and through all my questioning found out exactly what PR was all about, and realised it was just perfect for me.

The feature, and my conversations with the consultancies showed me that it is a really subtle marketing tool that can be used very effectively to sell products and services, and its real strength is that there is no hard sell in it at all. The third-party element takes care of that. All you are doing with PR is giving information relating to the product, service, company, charity, event, theory or whatever it is you are promoting, to journalists and/or other people of influence, and allowing them to report it as they please.

Grab attention and develop a thick skin

So, in these early days the tactics that I realised were needed were in presenting the material in such an enticing way as to whip up interest in the journalist enough to report it, and being able to grab their attention in the first few seconds on the phone and not be put off if they were terse and off-hand with you.

My telephone sales training taught me how to get to the point and captivate them early, and my experience of having hundreds of people put the phone down on me gave me a thick enough skin to not worry and keep going.

This is a necessary requirement if you are going to try and pitch stories to national journalists. It has been very valuable to me, as one of the big hurdles you need to get over in PR is having the confidence to call a journalist and pitch them your story in the first few seconds, before they brush you off as 'yet another PR' or someone trying to sell themselves rather than an interesting story.

News angle

You need to be able to hone down the news angle of your story to a very few sentences, and the reason you believe the journalist, and his/her readers/listeners would really be interested in it. And you need the courage to put it over to them however your call is being

received. If they reject you, just work your way down your target media list and call the next journalist.

Armed with this knowledge, and renewed enthusiasm about my career, I set off to find someone to employ me in PR. In those days it was usual to go into a consultancy at the very bottom and work your way up. Very few people had PR/Media/Marketing degrees or qualifications that took them in at a higher level, so I found a couple of lowest-of-the-low trainee jobs.

The first was at the European Law Centre (ELC), a company that was sold three months later. With my redundancy money safely deposited in the bank to help soak up my overdraft, I landed my first proper PR agency job.

It was with a small B2B multi-disciplined consultancy in central London called Minden Luby & Associates. One of the Directors was the husband of a girl I had made friends with at the ELC. She liked me and recommended me to him, and my PR career began.

PR (her third-party endorsement of me) had started working for me in my personal life too.

PUBLIC RELATIONS LESSON

PR is a very subtle, really effective marketing tool for promoting any business, service, product or person as its real strength lies in the fact that there is no hard sell involved at all.

1. PR is all about the value of third-party endorsement – getting someone else to tell the world how marvellous you are without you having to boast.

2. It is vital that you find, get to know, and regularly communicate your messages to those people who have the most influence on your target audience, so that they can do your selling for you.

3. You need to present your information to them in the way *they* want to receive it.

4. With no selling involved, you are merely giving information to these influential people, which they may find useful, allowing them to decide how they are going to use it.

5. For your material to be used, you need to be able to grab the journalist's attention immediately, either in the first few seconds of a phone conversation or the subject line of your press release.

CHAPTER THREE

Cleaning Up

> 'Next to doing the right thing, the most important thing is to let people know you are doing the right thing.'
>
> *John D. Rockefeller*

The marvellous world of case studies

Anyone who has ever worked with me, or who I have advised on using PR, will verify that I am totally obsessed with case studies and their use in your PR.

I first realised their value through working with my oh-so-sexy first two clients. One who made industrial floor cleaning machines, and the other who manufactured the industrial flooring on which they were used. Imagine my excitement after three years promoting these products to move to the Pepsi account in Sydney, promoting Michael Jackson's tour. More on that later.

These clients wanted to be featured regularly in their trade press – *Floors and Flooring Monthly* if I remember rightly. Heady days! As they did not make many new products, or even exciting additions to existing products

each year, the only way we could get coverage for them was by writing up a constant stream of different case studies of how businesses in all walks of life were using the products. I really enjoyed it, and I was genuinely interested in each new story and how these fairly unexciting products had affected their businesses.

One of my favourites was a greyhound-racing stadium in Wimbledon, which used a strong type of industrial flooring. I loved going to visit them with a photographer, interviewing them, and seeing how it all worked. Not sure I picked up any hot racing tips, though.

Another world – and such fun.

After my three years with them, we had a fantastic range of case studies all getting great coverage as the editor of *Floors and Flooring Monthly* knew he could rely on me for some good stories to fill his pages, his readers were saying they enjoyed reading them and the client was making sales.

I also realised you could gain added coverage by placing the case studies in the trade and local press of the company you were writing about. For example, *Dog-racing Monthly* and *Airport Facilities*, *Wimbledon Guardian* and *Crawley Observer* – or whatever their names were; I can't remember now.

Get forward looking

Another discovery I found out in these early days was the value of forward features in publications. I knew that *Floors and Flooring Monthly* was my most valuable trade publication for those two clients, so I had made it my business to get to know the editor and always called after I had sent a press release to check if he needed anything else and all was well. This also gave us a chance to chat about what he was working on and whether I might have any material from my clients that would help the articles.

He told me they had a set list of forward features for the year, around which they sold advertising, which made sense from my *Campaign* days. Though I was now the other side of the fence (never to go back), and as long as my material was relevant and sent within the deadline, I would get coverage in them.

I stuck to the list religiously, trying to make sure we were in every feature. Sometimes I created a storyline or found some angle in the clients' businesses that we could twist to fit the feature. They got some great regular coverage that way – and the journalist loved me, as he knew he could rely on me to help fill his pages.

This was my first taste of the importance of developing good relationships with your target journalists and helping them wherever possible. Much more on that later.

Blue-sky thinking

My PR Director at Minden Luby & Associates was a very witty, intelligent and feisty Irishman called Adrian. He worked hard and quickly in the mornings and pretty much took each afternoon off – after a few pints at lunchtime. He could think totally out of the box, and always encouraged me to do the same so that, seemingly from nowhere, he could come up with good news angles to use for clients, even when, to all intents and purposes, there were none. 'Fly by the seat of your pants, Lucy,' he would advise.

I would watch him with awe in client meetings, asking all sorts of questions: about the business and its future plans; the market in general; the personalities and hobbies of the employees; the charitable deeds of anyone associated with the company; events taking place locally and which were the local sports teams. Then he would sit back in his chair, take a deep breath, stretch up his arms, run his hands through his hair, and rattle off ideas for press releases that no-one else had even contemplated. I have used that technique so much over the years.

Adrian made sure he fully understood the problem before suggesting solutions. Most people offer solutions first and ask questions second.

He had a real Irish curiosity and a wonderful view of the world. He would see interesting aspects in people

and things that others would not – and be able to comment on and write about them wittily and sensitively. He was also confident enough to tell the client that their idea was nothing more than an advertisement and therefore no good for PR.

It meant that he could always find something interesting to write about for his clients. That is a real skill in PR as a journalist will not write about something that is a thinly disguised advertisement, or that has no relevance to his readers.

This was a valuable lesson in distinguishing between advertising and PR – summed up by Jean-Luis Gassee:

> 'Advertising is saying you're good, PR is getting someone else to say it for you.'

I took this skill into my own PR work and made sure I was always giving journalists a proper news story – even when my clients were asking me to do otherwise, and what they wanted me to promote was, really, straight out of a brochure or advertising copy. 'This is a really luxurious house, Lucy' or 'we are award winning developers, the journalists *must* want to write about us'. Whilst these statements were true they did not amount to a story with sufficient legs to get into a newspaper.

What I kept telling myself (and still do now in relation to marketing myself and my products and services) is that,

sadly, journalists do not care at all about my clients and their products. They only care if it is something that will interest their readers. So, I had to always be looking for the news angle that would turn a rather mediocre idea into something that a newspaper *would* want to report on.

'Why would anyone want to read about this?'

I also found out through my growing number of journalist friends, that this was a skill that many of my PR peers did *not* have, and which was therefore really irritating to the journalists who felt their time was being wasted on 'non-stories', and therefore did not give these stories any coverage. Interesting.

Adrian taught me that you need to always be asking yourself:

> 'Would I want to read about this in my trade or local paper, if I did not work for this company?'

It struck me again that this natural curiosity that I had really was very useful. If you try to find out more about the product, service or whatever it is you are promoting and look deeper into it – from outside the box too - ideas and angles present themselves to you.

And it is the same with case studies. You will find all sorts of interesting information if you keep asking and probing,

which might interest the journalist more than what they are actually doing with your product or service.

PR affects every aspect of life

When I eventually left Minden Luby, as we moved to Sydney with my husband's job, Adrian's letter of reference was my first light bulb moment to realising how PR really does affect every part of your life.

His comment that I was 'both liked and respected by everyone I worked with, and that the organisation that employed me would enjoy a very good return on its investment,' – made me realise that elements of my character that I used to take for granted were obviously of major benefit to my work as a PR and I should take note of that.

I realised that it was these qualities (such as befriending the journalists and helping with their forward features) that had got me so much coverage.

Armed with this knowledge I set off to fish in a much bigger pond, down under.

PUBLIC RELATIONS LESSON

Case studies are the fundamentals of third-party endorsement and it is therefore important for your PR that you are collecting, writing and pitching them to your target media on a regular basis.

Five essential tactics you should be employing in your PR strategies to ensure you have a constant stream of good case studies being prepared, and gaining coverage are:

1. Dig deep and ask lots of questions when you are collecting your information as there may be a more interesting story in the case study than just that they have used your product or service successfully.

2. Remember there are often other places for your case studies in addition to *your* local or trade press. They will be relevant to the local and trade media of the subject of the case study too.

3. Get the forward features lists of your target media and aim to be finding good case studies to fit into any relevant features for your business.

4 Think outside the box and always ask yourself if the story in the case study is newsworthy. If it isn't, find something to add to it to make it appealing to the media.

5 Never present a journalist with something that is not newsworthy to *his or her* readers. Case studies need to add something to the value of the story the journalist is going to be reporting.

CHAPTER FOUR

Taking Off Down Under

> 'A genuine leader is not a searcher for consensus but a moulder of consensus.'
>
> Martin Luther King, Jr.

Three years later, my husband and I moved to Australia with his job and my PR career really took off.

With permanent residency, later to become an Australian citizen, I worked for two consultancies in Sydney – Shandwick Australia and Holt Public Relations. The latter was Australia's largest PR consultancy with branches in every state and some fantastic clients.

In terms of the way these consultancies worked, and the calibre of the clients compared to Minden Luby, this was like taking my one-woman show from the village hall to the West End stage. I loved it.

In both companies, my clients were big Australia-wide or Global PLCs and they included Pepsi, pasta ready meals, Tabasco Sauce, Mortein Cockroach Spray, Ribena, Ampol petrol stations, Tubemakers of Australia (pipes etc),

computers, pens, Australian Rules Football and many others. The people I was working with were enthusiastic, bright and fun. The clients really stretched my skills and abilities and wow, did I learn a lot.

Shandwick Australia

I started at Shandwick as soon as we arrived. We were on a two-year contract, but ended up staying for nearly four years. As it was the down-under branch of one of the UK's major PR consultancies, it felt comfortable to start work for them while I got to know the Aussie way of doing things.

The owner of Shandwick Australia, Jim, was brilliant at crisis management. He had a sharp, clear mind and could see potential problems in our clients' procedures and systems that could have caused problems. And he was not shy at telling the client – in a professional manner of course, and thereby showing them the importance of creating a clear crisis management plan, in case one day the nightmare did hit.

It has been my experience since, that most business owners, particularly in the entrepreneur/small business/ start up world do not see the value of spending the time creating a crisis management plan. Instead they tend to adopt a more 'let's concentrate on building it up, and I am sure if anything goes wrong we will sort it out at

the time' approach to their business, which can have very bad consequences for them.

I have had many calls from small business owners asking if I can do an urgent project for them as 'a very bad story about us is about to hit the news' and they need to quash it fast. Sadly, with no plan in place, and the speed with which a negative story gets spread now, with social media (and our natural love of bad news), there is usually not much I can do by the time they have rung me.

It astounds me that people don't see the value of taking some time and expertise to protect the *marvellous reputation* that they have taken so much time to create.

As Warren Buffet says:

> 'It takes 20 years to build a reputation and five minutes to ruin it. If you think about that, you'll do things differently.'

At Shandwick, I was lucky to be part of a team putting together a crisis management plan for one of our major clients, who had offices across Australia and a big corporate profile. I learned that the plan needs to include identifying and co-ordinating a crisis management team who know exactly what their responsibilities are, and who have the necessary skills needed in a crisis.

With his clarity of mind and umbrella view of the client's business, Jim helped them (and me) really hone down what procedures, tasks, functions and therefore skills were needed to cover all the aspects of the crisis management plan: like crisis evaluation, damage limitation, product recall (if relevant), logistics, internal and external communications, general support, overseeing, updating and testing the crisis management processes. And more.

Luckily, we only had to activate a small part of the plan when I was there, and we were obviously involved in the communications process to major stakeholders and internally, but its lessons in preparation stayed with me.

A major change in my work life when we arrived in Sydney was making friends with a girl in the office who was part of a crew that raced yachts on the harbour every Wednesday evening. So instead of falling into the smoky, packed pub next door to the Minden Luby office on the way to the tube station, as we used to do most days after work in London, we would finish work bang on 5pm and be on the boat, on the beautiful Sydney Harbour, beer in hand, by 6pm.

I vividly remember my first birthday after arriving there. December the first. I swam in an unheated, salt water, outdoor pool under the Harbour Bridge in my lunch hour.

After several months at Shandwick I found the wonderful Holt Public Relations and made the move to them. Which was where the excitement really started.

Publicity stunts

Sir Richard Branson is a great proponent of publicity stunts, saying:

> 'Publicity is absolutely critical. A good PR story is infinitely more effective than a front page ad.'

He is always looking to find a stunt to get himself into the media.

At Holt, I learnt that if you can think imaginatively and creatively to find stunts that do not undervalue your business and personal values, then it really is a great way to get free editorial for yourself, especially if what you are trying to publicise is not particularly exciting or photogenic.

For example, one of my clients was Mortein Cockroach Spray. Literally just a can of spray – how boring is that? They were re-launching it with a different sort of packaging, and that was the story we had to publicise, with a brief to get them as much media coverage across Australia as we could.

My colleague Trudi put on a huge cockroach suit and we wedged ourselves and a photographer into the

tiny office kitchen. My drama degree came to the fore as I valiantly killed this giant monster with a few spurts of my wonderful Mortein spray.

The result achieved loads of press coverage with some amusing comments and lots of sales.

One of my early jobs with Holt PR was with the Pepsi team. They were always doing publicity stunts and fun promotions; at the time I arrived Michael Jackson was on tour throughout Australia, and Pepsi were sponsoring it.

Soon afterwards they sponsored the launch of Aussie rock star John Farnham's new album (remember him? The Voice. Great song), so the office was full of promotional gifts, goody bags, loud music for inspiration, and vast numbers of press releases and photos (no email and internet in those days, so everything was printed out and put in the post). And cans of Pepsi on every desk.

The Pepsi team was headed by Karen, the most energetic and bossy woman I had ever met. She seemed to have a can of Pepsi glued to one hand (until the end of the day when it was replaced with a glass of wine), and a fag to the other (smoking in the office was still allowed then).

She would whip us up into creating wild publicity stunts like getting a small plane to fly under the Harbour Bridge to launch John Farnham's album, with

accompanying music blaring out from the harbour walls. When an idea seemed good enough, one of us was sent off to research and organise it. She was an expert at delegation and would never take no for an answer. *She* loved the idea so it *would* work. Keep trying and talking to people, someone will help you get it sorted was her motto.

The result? Karen's clients got amazing free editorial and journalists loved her.

When it came to media relations, Karen was, again, a legend, and I learned masses from her. When she arranged these publicity stunts and events – which I remember as constant and dominating the office, but I guess in reality there were only two or three in my three years with Holt -she would work brilliantly with the target media so that she got her client on every news section of every radio, TV and print media in Australia.

I learned from her that you need to get your event bible ready: a central list of target media to work from, with *all* their contact details and a notes section for each of them. Every time anyone contacted one of these media, we had to put all the snippets we had found out about them into the notes (like they loved/ hated Michael Jackson's music, or they had another big event on that day but would try and come to ours, or they were on holiday but would get someone else

to cover, or it was their daughter's birthday so how could they forget the day?). This meant that when we called them next time, we could bring these snippets up in conversation, and the contact felt good that we had remembered, and we were really wanting *them* personally to attend our event.

It was so clever, methodical and at the same time personal and fun, and I have used this very successfully for several events. And of course it is *brilliant* for creating a database of information on your target media so you can build those vital long-term relationships with them. You really get to know them after this build up and can then go back to them with your other stories – and they will now value you as their ear-to-the-ground in your industry. You all know like and trust each other.

Karen taught me that you need to find many reasons to call them before the event to make sure that they have the date in their diaries and that they are whipped into the same excitement of the whole thing that we were made to feel in the office. So that by the time you reached the day of the event, there was no way these people were *not* going to attend, or at least cover it in their media, and it only needed another call first thing in the morning to book in the time for them to interview your client. They totally bought into the whole project and we didn't accept no for an answer.

Of course, we don't all have a project as exciting as the tour of a world-famous rock star to promote, but you can use the learning from this in your own businesses, whatever size.

The power of the press release

Right from the beginning, reading that feature in *Campaign*, I realised why the cornerstone of good PR is writing press releases – though it always irritates me that people who don't understand the huge power of the public relations world think that PR stands for press release and is the only marketing tool we have.

At each consultancy in which I have worked, and with every client from whichever type of business they were in, the first job has always been to set up a steady flow of press releases going out to the client's target media. Fundamental and vital.

For your own PR, if writing is not your thing I would strongly recommend you find a good copywriter and make sure you keep feeding them angles to prepare press releases for you, so that you can then spend your time placing the stories with your target journalists.

Formal press releases are important because:

1. Journalists are very busy and get overwhelmed by information coming at them every day, so receiving your material in a good, well-written press release format will make the difference between your story

making the front page or hitting the bin. They simply don't have time to trawl through your material looking for a reason to publish it. You have to lay it out for them in a format they recognise and include all the elements they will need to make it a good story for them.

2. When you put your story into a press release format it ensures you are giving the journalist exactly what he or she needs to create their article. Even if your story is picture-based and you have sent the journalist the image, they will always ask for a press release with all the details of what is happening in the photograph, and your contact information. So you must get it written first.

A press release for each activity

In every consultancy I've worked in, and in my own of course, we have regular monthly meetings with the clients, coming up with ideas and a comprehensive list of all the activities we have undertaken to do in the next month, each one with a press release attached to it.

This is such a good discipline for your business, as it forces you to be always looking for stories in your world, and communicating regularly with your target media. Once you've been forced to write your story idea down, you will be more inclined to make sure it gets published.

If journalists get used to receiving good, well-written press releases from you, which deliver them a story or comment that they can just lift and use then and there, they are going to look out for your name in their inbox and are more likely to use your material.

And of course, this works the other way too: badly crafted, non-newsworthy, salesy press releases will irritate them and they will avoid any further contact with you. Remember what my national journalist contacts told me about some of my PR colleagues?

One of the senior directors at Holt, Trevor, had previously worked as a very sharp news editor on *The Sun*, a similar paper to the UK one of the same name, with short stories, snappy headlines and no waffle.

I loved the way he thought about a news story and then wrote press releases for his clients, and I learned a lot from him. I've summarised the five most important points for you here. They are fundamental if you want to learn to write press releases that convert into column inches.

1. Get your angle and be newsworthy

I learned from my mistakes here. In these early days of my PR career I would often come up with ideas for press releases for my clients, show them to Trevor and have him lean back in his chair, light up another cigarette, raise an eye-brow and ask (just like Adrian had done at

Minden Luby): "Would you really want to read about this if you didn't work for this client?'

Which meant – this is rubbish, go away and think of something else.

It is such a good mantra to keep in your head when you are thinking about news stories and then actually writing the press release:

Would you really want to read about this if you didn't work in your business?

What *is* the news angle here and why would people want to read about this?

You must tailor your angle to the readers of the publication – think what they'd be interested in or the journalist will not see the point of using it. Create an angle if necessary and work your products or services into the press release to suit the tone and subject matter of the publication.

2. Create a punchy headline

Trevor was brilliant at headlines and always re-wrote mine. I would often give him my releases to read through and ask him to add the headline – like the sub-editors do in newspapers. It is so important to get this right, especially now that we email our releases to journalists. Ours need to stand out in their email stream, and compel them to start reading our stories.

Your headline is your first weapon in grabbing their attention so craft it carefully. Something that needs a second look and sounds unusual and exciting – a bizarre statistic, an unusual statement or a provocative question is always good.

Trevor taught me that the tools for this are:

❯ Focusing on the newsworthy angle.

❯ Using alliteration.

❯ Harmless innuendo (within reason).

❯ Analogies.

❯ Locality - if the story relates to a local person or place, get that in the headline too.

You can even write down 20 headline options and then choose the best. In this way, by the time you get to the 18th or 19th, you will have a good one because your brain is really into getting your message concise and tight. The fewer words the better.

3. WWWWWH

A really basic PR rule – and Adrian taught me this at Minden Luby. The first paragraph of any press release must summarise the essence of the entire story, answering:

Who, What, Where, Why, When and How?

You must start with whatever the newsworthy part is. Whether you have raised several thousand pounds or it's a new product or new premises or new person joining or you've had the Duchess of Cambridge visiting your business. Whatever it is that should be in the first paragraph.

Also in your press release you need to have a call to action, either in that first paragraph or near the end, depending on how important it is. If the whole point of your press release is announcing a competition or incentive, then that is what you will put in your first paragraph, and the call to action at the end will tell people how to enter the competition.

The call to action might just be to ring you up for further information, so therefore you will need all your contact details (one telephone number and website – don't fuss the journalist with too much).

4. Format of release and Notes to the Editor

When you have finished your release, put:

- Ends -

Notes to the Editor:

Give a contact name, phone number and email address for the person the journalist can get in touch with if they need more information.

You can also put more background information in here about the people and events mentioned in the release, and references for the statistics and facts you have used, noting which publications or documents they have come from with a hyperlink if possible.

Here you can also give a fuller description of what your business does (as, in order to keep it concise, you will only have mentioned the business name in the press release). Also say what else you can offer – like an interview with someone in the business, a case study and more photos.

A Notes to the Editor section makes your press release look more professional.

5. Be clear, no jargon and include a quote

Again, through trial and error in these early consultancy days, I learned that the total aim of media relations is to make the journalist's life as easy as possible. Then he or she is more likely to use your press releases. It's called making them oven ready.

Trevor used to get the red pen out to any of my releases that were not clear in their message, cutting out waffle and any industry jargon. And, as I always did in these consultancies, and my colleagues and I do now in Marvellous PR, no matter how senior I became, it's important that you get someone to read through your press release before you send it out to

make sure it makes sense, is interesting and has no silly mistakes.

I learned from my follow-ups with journalists, after I had sent out the press release and was ringing to see if they needed anything else to make it usable, that they always want useful supporting statistics and quotes to give it some kind of human angle. So if you are a step ahead and have already included the quote and relevant stats for them, they are much more likely to use your press release than your competitor's.

Know your onions

Isn't it amazing that certain events, way back in your life, stick out so clearly in your mind that you can remember every element of them – and yet what you had for supper last night is a mystery this morning?

I believe that is to do with fate, the universe kind of putting a highlighter under that event, and what you learned from it at the time, so that you can keep referring to it through your life. I did say earlier I am a fatalist and I believe things happen for a reason, and if you are tuned into them, you will realise why, grasp the learning or the meaning and let it influence your life in the right direction.

We often need to think about something at least three times before it gets retained in our long-term memory,

but, if a lesson is associated with fear it will get into long-term memory the first time.

My onions and oranges nightmare at Holt was one of those. What I learned I still find useful today.

One of my clients was Tabasco Sauce. How were we going to promote Tabasco Sauce – and create press releases for them? We decided to get a chef to come up with some nice recipes for us, we wrote them out, photographed the finished food, obviously stressing that it had Tabasco Sauce in it, and sent it out with the contact name and address of the company that sold Tabasco Sauce (my client), to over 600 newspapers across Australia. All the towns sold Tabasco Sauce, so the target audience was huge.

One such press release was for stuffed oranges, filled with rice, laced with Tabasco Sauce.

We sent out the release and photograph and then thought no more about it until we started to get our press cuttings back.

One after another the cuttings said something to the effect of 'Samuel Taylor (the client) doesn't seem to know its oranges from its onions as it has just sent us a recipe for stuffed onions – how revolting is that?'

With trepidation, I checked the press release we had sent out and sure enough it read: 'Take six large onions' not 'take six large oranges!'

Oh my God. So we had to phone 600 press contacts urgently, begging them to find the press release, change it to oranges, or at least run a correction in their publication the following week if they had already printed it with onions. It was awful. I felt totally stupid, but I think we saved the day.

So what are the five big learnings that I took from this mix up?

1. They can report it how they like
In a democratic country, with a free press, journalists can report things how they want (if they are not slanderous or libellous, of course) – and they did. Hence the how revolting comment about the onions.

2. You never see copy first
Journalists are often not allowed to show you what they are going to publish before it is filed, so you will rarely be sent a proof of their articles, for you to check the facts. So, it is important that you double check what you are sending out before it goes and be happy to stand by any comments you have made in your press release.

3. Get to know your journalists
It's vital to develop that good relationship with your target journalists so that if anything you would not want reported does get sent to them accidentally, you will be

able to rely on their better judgement not to publish it. Also, you will have their personal contact details so that you can call them quickly in case of emergency.

4. Good releases get printed word for word
If your press release is well written, the journalist (particularly on local and trade publications) may well reproduce it word for word - and the better the relationship they have with you, the more likely they are to do so , because they will trust you. Which is usually a brilliant thing as they are writing exactly what you want them to say – until you make a mistake like I did.

5. Never complain
You must never ever go back to a journalist once they've done an article and complain - unless of course they are being libellous. Apart from that, it is up to them. This is free editorial. I've had a lot of clients over the years who have complained at me because the journalist has written a description of their product or business in a way they, the journalist, sees it, not how the client would want it worded. You can obviously go back to the journalist if they have got their facts wrong, like we did with this onions and oranges saga, and politely and apologetically beg them to help you, and they will probably run an apology, and correction.

PUBLIC RELATIONS LESSON

In case the worst happens, every business should have a crisis management plan, with clearly laid out objectives, procedures and responsibilities including a communications strategy to key stakeholders via your target journalists.

Working with these journalists and building strong, respectful relationships with them is fundamental for good PR generally. Here are five essentials to remember when working with journalists:

1 They can report the story how they like. No money is changing hands and they are free to write their opinions and versions of your story.

2 You will rarely be allowed to see copy before it is published so never ask to see it.

3 You need to get to know your target journalists, how they work and how they want to receive information.

4 Well-written press releases generally get printed word for word.

5 You must never complain about how your story has been covered unless it is libellously wrong.

CHAPTER FIVE

School's Out

> 'Either write something worth reading
> or do something worth writing about.'
>
> Benjamin Franklin

We now fast forward seven years and re-join my PR career in Luxembourg.

We moved back to the UK with our three children, living in a quintessentially English village near Guildford in Surrey, called Shamley Green. Complete with two great pubs, a beautiful village green where my husband played cricket for the village, a sweet village shop and stunning views of the surrounding hills and countryside.

I settled happily into life as a stay-at-home mum with no thoughts whatsoever of returning to work. Four years later, we moved to Luxembourg, following my husband's job again, and found ourselves in a very British community. My daughters attended St George's International School (locally known as The British School) and I found myself among parents who moaned constantly about the state

of the education and facilities at the school compared with the huge fees.

When we started at the school there were 40 children aged between three and twelve, in about three classes, from a range of different countries, some not speaking much English, others about to return to a place at Eton. A mixed bunch, with a very varied teaching staff, equally broad selection of parents – and relatively no facilities.

After a few months there, it became obvious that if you wanted extra things for the children, you had to do it yourself. As I am a great joiner-in, I soon found myself helping with loads of things.

Three of us prepared the *Dragon News* school newsletter which went out to parents and children each term (the school was called St George's – dragon – see what we did there?) and we took turns to be on the PTA giving the poor owners a hard time about the lack of music/drama/art/sports/you-name-it facilities at the school for the exorbitant fees they were charging.

In one such PTA meeting, the owner of the school said, 'We cannot afford the extra staff and facilities for the activities you want. We do not have enough fees coming into the school.'

To which I replied (in a way reminiscent of the telephone sales patter I had been taught all those years ago), 'So,

if we could get you more children into the school would you promise us more facilities?'

'Yes of course, Lucy. Are you offering?'

'Yes, I am. You need PR and a solid marketing strategy. If I can bring in two friends to help me, would you employ us, one day per week, to really market the school properly?'

'Yes please. When can you start?'

So began the next stage of my PR career.

The results of instigating, planning and implementing a proper PR and marketing strategy for St George's School were phenomenal and proof of how PR can have an amazing effect on the bottom line and return on investment of a business.

I was back in PR employment, even if only one day a week, in term time only, getting my teeth into how to raise the profile and image of the school and bring children in as fast as possible.

I asked my two great friends to join me, Diana a highly organised and efficient Dutch woman who spoke half a dozen languages fluently and was happy to set up the systems and organise the back-up to it all; and Veronica, who has sadly died since, but whose influence on our work at St George's and, importantly, on my own

life, cannot be emphasised enough. As a hard-nosed recruitment consultant in the UK who had set up her own business and successfully sold it, she not only had a brilliant telephone sales technique but could also close the sale. The word 'no' did not exist in her vocabulary.

The team set to work and I was in charge of all the PR and marketing.

Luxembourg News

The first job was to work out which press we were dealing with. This turned out to be relatively easy – there was only one English speaking regular monthly publication, *Luxembourg News*. My next vital task was to read this publication really carefully, work out what kind of stories they covered, who wrote them, and then get to know the editor so that she knew, liked and trusted me.

Next, I had to find angles to create press releases to send to her every month. We managed it, with loads of lateral thinking, good photography and strong community involvement.

This was the big learning for me. It was the first time that I realised the value of being involved in, sponsoring, organising and then publicising, community events and activities.

Community events and activities

The PR value behind this is partly the obvious publicity it generates through editorial and photographs, but also, and almost more powerfully, the third-party endorsement element it gives, in terms of the Law of Association.

For example, I organised for the school to sponsor and have a stand at, the annual British Ladies' Club Car Boot Sale, in a central square in Luxembourg, attended by every English-speaking member of the Luxembourg community. I did the same at the annual village fete, held in one of the bigger villages outside the city. Both events raised funds for well-known charities, so we had added goodwill and PR from being associated with them – as well as being seen to support the British Ladies' Club, the most influential English-speaking organisation in Luxembourg.

After 18 months' hard work, we had a huge leap in enquiries from people reading the editorials and attending the events, and who were then converted to pupils with Veronica's super sales techniques. We were also able to take hard copies of all our editorials to show companies whose employees were coming to Luxembourg and might be interested in their children attending the school.

'Look how important we are,' we would say, 'Luxembourg News just can't write enough about us.'

When we were preparing to leave Luxembourg to return to the UK, Tony Barlow, the owner of the school, reflected that when he recruited me, the school was suffering from falling enrolment and a poor image within the community and was close to financial insolvency. 18 months of our PR and marketing work later, the image of the school had improved dramatically, enrolment doubled and it was now on a sound financial footing.

Today there are 750 children in their own purpose-built school buildings. Brilliant.

Another school, another PR role

Four years later we returned to the UK. Back to Surrey to a bigger house in a different village further away from Guildford, called Wormley. All three children ended up together at St Hilary's School in Godalming.

I was not expecting to go back to work. The children were still young, four, six and eight, I was happy being at home with them, and I was lucky my husband had a good job so I could afford to do this.

Day after day in the school car park, waiting with the other mums for the children to come out, all I heard were negative comments about the school, and how other schools were so much better and 'all my friends are looking at them and thinking of taking their children away from St Hilary's' etc.

You have probably heard exactly the same, and it irritated me. I did not like to hear people moaning about somewhere that I had chosen as a good resource for my children – and I also felt strongly that their opinions were wrong, and only formed by peer pressure.

The communications' channels between St Hilary's, the parents, and the outside world were not good. There was no parent-teacher newsletter, no regular articles in the local papers and no one knew how well the school was doing and all the wonderful things the teachers and children were achieving.

As you can imagine, I couldn't let it lie, and eventually found myself sitting on the comfy sofa in the head teacher's office, along with the bursar, explaining what I was hearing all the time in the car park, what I had done in terms of PR for St George's and why I really felt they needed some urgent help with their image, if not greater numbers of pupils.

I was working in PR again.

I was very part-time, and again my job entailed finding the angles, writing the releases, and ensuring we had photographs of every event, however small, as they could be combined with others in an article that could end up on the front page of the local paper several times a term.

The profile of the school, both externally with new/ prospective parents, and internally with current parents, leapt up as a result.

Snap it all

I learned at St Hilary's that even if your event is very small and seemingly unimportant, it is always worth having a professional photographer to take your photos, as the results are so much clearer and more interesting and properly tell the story.

It is vital that you provide a photograph for journalists to accompany your press releases, even if your business is not photogenic, and you are merely commenting on something. If it's just a comment, the photograph should be of the person commenting of course.

I also discovered that, wherever possible, it was better for us to call the picture desk at the local paper, before editorial, on some occasions, and get them to put the event into their diary.

'It is such a great photo opportunity' we would say. And once the paper's photographer had taken the picture, they were much more likely to run the story. Canny, and very useful.

Photographs can make or break the chances of your story being used. So do adhere to these fundamentals:

❯ They need to be high resolution (between 1 – 10MB).

❯ Always give an informative caption with all names, and job titles where appropriate, in full and spelled correctly, from L to R.

❯ They need to be professionally taken.

❯ There should not be too many people in the picture.

❯ The photograph must help tell the story you are writing about.

❯ If it is about the opening of a building, then the photographs need to be close ups of the people cutting the ribbon or whatever, absolutely honing in on them.

❯ If it is a new product then you must have the new product either being used or in a nice background and the image always needs to be clean and clear, illustrating what you are saying.

Always check that everyone in the photograph is happy to be in it. Some people do not realise that, even when pictures are being taken professionally, they are going to appear in the press. So make sure you have everyone's permission, you have spelled all their names and job titles correctly, and everything is in order before you send the picture to the journalist.

PUBLIC RELATIONS LESSON

Implementing a well-thought-out PR and Marketing Strategy will make a real impact on your business and its bottom line, if undertaken consistently and with laser focus on who your target audience is and who their influencers are.

Your Strategy needs to include:

1. A good quality image or infographic to accompany every story.

2. Finding exactly which media your target audience is getting its information from, working out who is writing it, what they need and getting them to know, like and trust you.

3. Community events and organisations that you can be involved with throughout the year.

4. Stories and angles written up as press releases which can be communicated regularly to your target media each month.

5. If your product or business is photogenic then take as many pictures as you can, for potential photo press releases, and encourage the picture editor of your local paper to attend any events to take their own pictures.

CHAPTER SIX

Property Builds Career

> 'Public relations specialists make
> flower arrangements of the facts,
> placing them so the wilted and less
> attractive petals are hidden by
> sturdy blooms.'
>
> *Alan Harrington,*
> *Wales international footballer*

At a dinner party with fellow St Hilary's parents I met a property developer whose daughter was in Hannah's class. He asked what work I had done before I had children, and what I enjoyed about the job. As soon as I mentioned PR his eyes lit up and he suggested I meet his PR consultant, Nikki, who ran Property House Marketing, a PR consultancy purely for property clients. Apparently she was looking for people to work for her.

I assured him I had no intention of going back to work. I was having fun helping raise the profile of St Hilary's, and my top priority, and what I loved most, was being a mum and at home for the children. Thanks, but no thanks.

He persisted. 'Just come to my office and meet her. You never know where it might lead and there is absolutely no commitment on either side to work together. It just might work sometime for both of you.'

I went for coffee, enjoyed her company, the clients sounded really interesting and she very generously gave me lots of flexibility to work the hours I could around the children.

And so began a new career in the exciting media world of bricks and mortar. One that I am still heavily involved in 16 years later and absolutely love.

I have also kept referring to his comment, 'You never know where it might lead,' ever since, whenever something is suggested to me which seems slightly out of my comfort zone, or a potential diversion from the path I have created for myself. I now give everything a go, and do not dismiss anything until I am sure it is not going to help me. Fate is looking out for us, I believe, and you never know where the next lifeline, which will take you closer to your goal, is going to come from.

Punters love property

Property House's clients were estate agents, property developers, national house builders, architects, interior designers – anyone who needed to get their story,

houses, and profile into the property supplements of the local and national media and property trade press.

Although I had already realised the value of monitoring the news and having my clients comment on anything relevant to their industry, I had not really had the chance to get so involved in it, and so regularly, as I did when I entered the property world.

The British are a nation obsessed with property. TV programmes about where we live, how we live in it and how we can improve it, are appearing (and disappearing) every day. There are also hundreds of print and on-line titles, the property supplements of the national papers are always very well read, and rarely does a day go by without some comment, somewhere in the media, popping up from a property pundit speculating on 'how this will affect the property market, and house prices.'

There is always work in the world of property PR, even in recessions. And it is so interesting.

I quickly realised PR for property works on the same formula as all the other industries I had worked in for my PR clients. It is still all about finding the angle, interesting the journalists with it, writing good pitches and press releases, providing fantastic photographs and developing good relationships with the target media.

No apologies for repeating myself. This cannot be stressed enough if you want to use PR to get yourself those valuable free column inches and raise your profile – and bottom line.

In addition to this, a lot of my work, as it has since continued, involved responding quickly to journalists' requests for comments on what was happening in the news. Providing interesting opinions, speculations and alternative ways of viewing the story, that, preferably, some other pundits will not have thought of.

I have always been lucky to work with interesting, well-informed clients and the coverage we have achieved, from reacting fast to what is happening in the news and getting our comments, in a well-written format, to the right person before their deadline, has paid us dividends.

Relationships with journalists are symbiotic

Until this point, I don't think I understood how symbiotic the relationship between journalists and PRs is and what this really means to me, and my clients. I had realised how important it was to make good relationships with them, but the light bulb moment I had when I started working at Property House was that my journalist relationships were actually more important to me than the relationships with my clients.

Let me explain.

A huge proportion of national property journalists are freelance. Which means that they work across the board for several national titles as well as some of the trade press. So, they can really help you get your story into a range of media, as well as having a choice of publications to choose from to find the best fit for your particular angle.

For example, one of my clients had a house for sale in central London. A typical white stucco-fronted property. Nothing particularly exciting about the bricks and mortar element to be honest, but owned by a young, totally mad milliner, who filled it with beautiful hats of many colours.

So the story was really about her and her business. Who she worked for (the glitterati of London) and how she used her house to work from. It was very pictorially led (the picture that made the cover of the newspaper was of her on the front steps, surrounded by fantastically creative hats and wearing bright stripy knee length socks and a colourful mini skirt). My freelance journalist friend, Cheryl Markosky, and I decided it was perfect for the *Mail on Sunday*.

She approached the editor with the idea and they ran it as a cover story and across the whole of Page Two. It would not have worked in *The Times*, for example, which was the paper we were originally aiming for, or at most it would only have got a small mention, and the freelancer who wrote about it for me, knew this,

worked for both, and found the right home for it where it would get the most coverage.

These journalists are as wedded to property as the PRs, clients and their readers. Which means that a lot of them have been writing for the same publications for years and will carry on doing so. Whereas clients, tho still remaining in the general property world, tend to move around within the industry, going to new companies with different demographics sometimes, who will probably have their own PRs, and/or setting up on their own (with no budget for PR).

Of course, I have clients who have been with me for years and years, and I have never lost a client due to bad feeling between us. However, if I were to lose a journalist's trust and relationship, I have lost a highly valuable asset for all my clients, possibly forever.

Journalists must know, like and trust you

I understood that working with journalists is exactly the same as with any other contacts: they need to know, like and trust you in order to work successfully with you. They want to find reliable sources to provide newsworthy stories, interesting angles and high-resolution images quickly and efficiently – to help them do their job.

In return, you want to get your stories run and be recognised as a contact for expert commentary. It is

simple, but not everyone seems to grasp this fundamental and important principle of PR.

It had been over 10 years since my Minden Luby days. The Ab Fab image of the long boozy lunch resulting in reams of press coverage, which really did happen when I first started in PR, was long gone. The world had changed, and the way journalists worked and got their news had changed too. This is still the case.

I found that then, as now, most journalists don't want to be your best friend or have a good lunch just for the sake of it. By all means offer to buy them lunch, coffee, breakfast or drinks at the end of their working day, but you have to make absolutely sure you have something good to offer them.

Do not waste their time and always give them the story as an exclusive. Nothing seals a relationship with a journalist better than a good story. A journalist who walks away from a meeting without a story feels cheated because then they will have to work even harder to find another story, having wasted several hours with you.

Shopping list of stories

That's when I learned the value of the shopping list for journalists. We used to create a long list of possible stories, from all our clients, giving them actual headlines for added impact. We would then offer the list to the

national journalists we met asking them to pick the story(ies) they wanted to pursue with us, assuring them that they would have them as exclusives if they took them through to publication. It worked brilliantly.

The more I got to know the freelance property journalists, the more I understood how it all worked. This principle is especially true for them as they are competing with their peers for space in the media. They need to please their editors so if you help them get commissions by delivering a great angle, you'll boost their bank accounts. Which will definitely endear you to them.

A journalist will be paid by the editor of the section for which he or she is writing the article. The PR will be paid by their client. So it is in the journalist's interest to be friendly with you because you are going to give them the stories in the first place. And the better the stories, the more likely they are to be published and the more money they will get. Consequently, the more likely the journalists are to be noticed and used by editors of other publications.

Suddenly they will have a range of different places to put their stories, which again, could be helpful to you. I began to see this happening more often, the more freelancers I was working with and the more frequently my stories were appearing in the wider press. Everyone was happy.

If you maintain a helpful relationship with your target journalists, they will use your material and will try and get you into almost any story they are writing because they can rely on you.

The mindset you need is always to be looking to *help* your target journalists with what they are writing, rather than focusing on *your* motivations all the time and thinking, 'I need to get my story in the press.'

I maintained the mantra of: 'I must help the journalist with *their* story, no matter what *my* story is'. And then when I was pitching stories to journalists I didn't feel I was selling to them, and they responded by helping me to get coverage for some of my more tricky stories.

PUBLIC RELATIONS LESSON

Good PR is following a formula, which can be used in any industry – and in our personal lives: finding the angle which will interest the journalists (or other influencers), preparing a good pitch to sell it to them, and developing really good relationships with your target media (or influencers) so they trust you. Here are five important things to remember about those relationships:

1 They are actually the most important relationships for you as the journalists/influencers will be there for you even when your clients and customers are coming and going in your life.

2 The relationship is symbiotic – they need you as much as you need them.

3 The *Ab Fab* boozy lunch is no more. By all means, meet up with them so they get to know you, but always give them a good story to take away then and there.

4 Always have the mind-set of how you can help the journalist with their story – not how you can get *your* story used. Subtle difference.

5   Really get to know the media you want to get into so that you can suggest to your journalist contacts new columns where the stories you are creating together could be used. That is helpful to them too.

CHAPTER SEVEN

Thatcher Meets Prescott

> 'It takes 20 years to build a reputation and five minutes to ruin it. If you think about that, you'll do things differently.'
>
> *Warren Buffet*

By now it was clear to me that in the world of PR i.e. third-party endorsement, it is *not* about you, the client, or their business, it is about getting a good relationship with those who will affect the opinions of your target audience. So that they naturally want to tell the world about you, your client or their business.

I learnt to word it that way with my target journalists. Approaching them with offers like: 'I want to help you. What can I, with the access I have to experts in the industry, do to get you a good story?'

Or: 'I see there is a column in xxxxxx, can I help you get a commission for a story in that?'

This took the pressure off the journalist to find the full story by the deadline. I could make sure my client got

a good slice of the copy and was in control of it and everyone was happy.

My work with these journalists helped me discover another valuable skill about PR – which has got me some great editorial hits over the years.

Keep up – call them regularly

With property features running weekly in the national newspapers, TV and radio programmes, there were so many stories flying around. It was, and still is, really important to make sure the journalists do not forget you and use someone else's houses and comments in their pieces.

So, I made it a routine to call my top journalist contacts, the ones who were writing regularly in all the big titles, every week to check what they were writing about – or just thinking about.

I often found they were delighted to chat with me, as they just needed an extra angle to make their idea work and talking to me about what I could help them with from my clients, or general research, got them there.

Of course, I needed to use all the self-development skills, that I had a passion for learning and putting into practice, as these calls needed to be full of energy and focussed on the journalist, and also end up making sure

I achieved the result I was after: that the journalists use my clients and material in their stories somehow.

Connect on a personal level

I also understood the value of learning what the journalists were really interested in, outside their property writing. Hobbies, children, holidays, sports interests, even what schools they went to (one of my contacts went to Cheltenham Ladies' College which proved helpful for our relationship). This allowed us to connect on another level, as well as our work, which then made it even easier to pitch my ideas to them.

For example, I had to pitch an important story for one of our clients to the Editor of the Home section in the *Sunday Times*, who was quite difficult to get through to. Even the freelance journalists struggled. We had invited her to a press lunch that we had arranged in London for some clients, and I was lucky enough (though terrified) to sit next to her. Suddenly I got my chance to speak to her properly, as something came up about *The Archers* and I have been an *Archers* fan all my life. Result. She mentioned something to do with one of the current story lines and I replied, in my best west country farmer's accent, because I knew what she was talking about, and wanted to make her laugh. She loved it and we got on well as we chatted and laughed away about Eddie, Joe, Lillian, Kenton, The Bull and all the characters we love to hate.

A day later, I rang her to pitch my story for *The Sunday Times'* Home section. As usual, she did not give me much time to say anything, until I butted in: 'Hi it's Lucy, you remember, *The Archers* fan?' And she suddenly relaxed completely and replied, 'Oh Lucy, yes, how are you?' After a few minutes discussing last night's episode, I pitched my story, and she wanted to see the press release.

I had not lied to her, or conned her into looking at my material. I had just found something we had in common, and as a result she warmed to me.

From one-man-band to corporate sale

Michael Parry-Jones, an estate agent whom Nikki had known for a while (she wrote the property page for the local *Surrey Advertiser*, and consequently knew everyone locally in property), asked us to help him launch his new agency, Parry Jones. He had a good following in Surrey and was starting up on his own in a tiny office with no staff, minimal marketing, and just one house on the books to sell.

He and I got on brilliantly; we were the same age with the same outlook on life, PR and how it all worked, and we ended up doing some fantastic work.

We met each month and focussed on one house at a time, choosing the one that was best for PR. I would go

round the house, searching for any unusual angles or quirky bits of history about it, talk in depth to the owners and eventually a hook (or two) would emerge.

For example, one couple had spent a huge amount of money on a really contemporary, state of the art kitchen, in an otherwise relatively unexciting looking house in a quiet residential street. So the angle (which got us front cover and two inside pages in the *Sunday Times* via my freelance friend, Fred Redwood) was 'why did they do it? How did they do it? How much did they spend? How do they live in it? Did they expect to get this money back on the sale?'

Readers love those through-the-keyhole stories.

One story leads to another

I worked on my contacts to get each house as much coverage as possible, looking at which papers and writers would suit it best and gathering all the various elements to make it a commission for them – as well as getting Michael mentioned in as many relevant commentary pieces as I could.

I absolutely love this side of PR. It uses imagination and creativity and is so rewarding when it comes together, matching the right angle, with the right journalist and the right publication and seeing the finished story in print.

I quickly realised that one success built on another with my journalists. We would finish one story and, as I would thank them for their help getting such great coverage for us (very important. You should always thank journalists for using your material), I was able to run the bones of the next one past them. And they were happy to work on it with me, as they realised we would get a good end result for both of us. It worked brilliantly and also helped raise my profile amongst the national property journalists, resulting in them recommending me to new clients. Great PR for me.

I learned so much from working with Michael and following his career, and he is a perfect example of how using PR for the long-term, and trusting in its incredible power to build your brand and expertise, can help you achieve your financial, and personal goals.

In his case this meant realising his ambitions to retire in his mid-50s and spend time with his family and travelling (a grown up word for holidaying).

It was a great relationship with Michael as he totally believed in the power of PR and used it to build up his profile and brand as an estate agent in the top end of the Surrey market, from scratch, enabling his businesses to compete with global international brands such as Knight Frank, Savills, Hamptons, and Strutt and Parker.

He always kept a very 'tight ship'. Twice he ran his business (setting up again after being bought out the

first time) in a delightful converted stable, in a small village, with minimal overheads.

As he was competing at the top end of the property market, his major competitors had huge offices of staff across the country and big matching marketing budgets. They were spending thousands each month on advertising and although he could not, and did not want to, compete with that, he also knew that being mentioned in *editorial* was worth around 500 times the cost of an advertisement, due to the third party endorsement and the power of association it gave from the national journalist writing the article.

People (his target audience) read articles in the property sections of *Country Life*, *The Times*, *Sunday Times*, *Telegraph*, *Daily Mail* and (in Michael's case) the *Surrey Advertiser*, much more than they read advertisements. He knew that if he were seen regularly commenting on the Surrey market, where best to buy, how to prepare your house for sale, with examples of his properties for sale alongside the article and comments from happy clients who had worked with him, the boost to his profile and brand would be phenomenal. And it was.

He decided to use his very limited marketing budget on doing PR, convinced it would be the tool to reach his goal of establishing his business and being the leading local estate agent of top end property in Surrey. He was right. The hundreds of column inches he secured in many

national media, as well as a constant stream of local editorial, meant that the return on his PR investment was far more than if he had bought advertisements.

National journalists, used to dealing with the big national estate agents, often commented that he must have a team of staff and a very busy agency, as 'you seem to be everywhere, in all the features'. When in fact he was working from his small office, using just his phone, his trusty black book and lots of PR to make sure that a story and/or commentary on the market was in every relevant media, every week.

His presence in the local and national media was so constant, and his profile so strong that after only a couple of years on his own, he was approached by a national agency who wanted a presence themselves in Guildford. The combination of the local profile and national brand worked incredibly well and when Michael left after five years, the office was the top performer within the area and the company. Top marks to PR, networking and profile.

A year later he re-emerged onto the market with a new business name, but the same black book of contacts, same small village office, couple more staff, and the same minimal marketing budget.

Again, he concentrated on PR and networking, building up the new brand in exactly the same way as before. This time, after six years, Michael merged the business with

a lettings company to create a larger multi-disciplined business with a strong high street presence.

Michael's dedication to PR meant that he became known among the national and local property journalists as someone they could trust for immediate commentary and help in creating their stories, with the result that his houses gained more valuable coverage than his competitors, allowing him to achieve higher prices for his clients. Good news all round.

As well as constant media activity to keep his name, and that of his business, in front of his target audience in the publications they were looking at, Michael used other PR tools to lift his profile and ensure his business was always on top of mind whenever his target audience decided they wanted to move house. He carefully selected, and sponsored, local sports, school and social events that his target audience attended, and was always networking in the right places. Thus, the people he wanted to attract were constantly linking him to the events and organisations in their lives, which strengthened their trust in his brand and meant they naturally brought their houses to him to sell.

Being old school, Michael took a long time to be convinced of the value of technology over the good old-fashioned little black book of contacts. And even when he did eventually put them onto his computer, he still contacted them personally, on the phone, on a regular basis to

check how they were going, whether they were thinking of moving and, if they were, he could find them the perfect house.

This was also a form of PR. His clients knew, liked and trusted him from his regular contact with them, which meant they stayed with him and didn't stray to his competitors.

Lessons in event-planning and story-making

Another important client at that time was Copthorn Homes, a branch of the national house-builder, Countryside Properties, set up to build architecturally exciting and unusual developments around the country. We were given one project to launch – a very unusual and architecturally challenging site in Harlow, Essex, called Abode at Newhall.

The story of this launch could be a book in itself. It was full of ups and downs and new experiences for me, and so successful that a year or so after it, during the time after Nikki and I had gone our separate ways, the owners of the land on which Copthorn were building looked me up and asked me to work for them on my own. They, together with Michael Parry-Jones, were my major clients for several years as I set up my own consultancy from home.

The essence of the project was so interesting, and heaving with great PR stories. The landowners had inherited the large estate, Newhall in Harlow, and decided to sell it off in parcels, rather than the whole lot to one developer. Unusually, they were selling to developer-architect partnerships, to build out each section with new ideas and designs but all keeping within a strong master plan of colours, textures and general infrastructure of the site.

They had already sold the first parcel to Barratt, and the second one to Copthorn who were working with architects Proctor and Matthews, which was a totally different, very modern and imaginative development of houses and apartments. The designs of the development, called Abode, included using lots of glass and steel and even had some thatch on some of the houses.

I was given the project of organising the launch of Abode, working with Nikki. It was a big event, involving lots of interested parties, all of whom had their own agendas, ideas and people needing to be included (and managed). We organised it in a field (muddy, uneven, no electricity or running water) close to the development, which was then only a few houses, so we needed a marquee and outside catering. I learned so much about planning PR events from Nikki whose events are always amazing.

A major part of the planning, as I had seen in action with Karen in Australia and her Pepsi events, was to

have a central running list of absolutely everything that needed to be done, covering all eventualities (weather, transport, illness, breakdowns, no-shows, etc.), every possible photographic opportunity and how it would be staged and managed.

Each element was assigned to someone to undertake, regularly updated, then double-checked and overseen by Nikki or me. Goodness knows how many times those lists were amended, but they were vital and meant we were prepared for anything to happen, with the right response. And the event was a huge success.

Our major coup (and headache) was getting John Prescott, Deputy Prime Minister at the time, to agree to officiate at the launch. With such a well-known VIP attending, the coverage was going to be good, but we were bowled over with how brilliant it ended up being.

The fact that so many different people were involved in the project meant that we had a lot of different story angles to offer to the press. So we were able to invite, and secure the attendance of (very tricky at an out of London venue) almost every property supplement in the national, regional and local media – print, TV and radio.

Normally when you have a good story, you have to offer it as an exclusive to a national publication or broadcast media, as they do not like to be running something exactly the same as their competition.

However, with Abode's launch we managed to get them all there to our muddy field in Essex, with their own angles to cover, and they all went away happy. A great result.

Loads went wrong on the morning of the event, but everything turned out fine. Guests survived the marquee which ended up being sited in the wrong place, with wonky floor boards placed on bare mud as the contractor had made a mistake in his planning, and they raved about the development at the time and for many months, and years afterwards.

Prescott meets Thatcher

Some of the media focussed on John Prescott and what Newhall stood for in relation to the future of the housing market; some focussed on the first resident there who was also at the event for journalists to interview; some focussed on the masterplan and its many elements for creating a new and sustainable community; others looked at the imaginative architectural and building designs, or at the story of the landowners and their vision.

There was so much to say, and we had spent so much time working out the angles, the photo opportunities and how it could all work, that the results were amazing. We had wanted a photograph of Mr Prescott meeting

the man who had put the thatch on the roofs – giving us the caption: **Prescott meets Thatcher** – but we couldn't quite stage that one.

Liaising with Mr Prescott's office taught me a lot too. First, we were not allowed to tell anyone he was attending, which made persuading the media to attend quite a tricky job. My earlier telephone sales techniques had to come to the fore – as well as now relying on the good relationships I was building with my national journalist contacts.

Then his timings kept changing, which meant our carefully-planned schedules and lists had to be super-flexible to accommodate him. We weren't sure what time he was arriving and his staff told us he could not stay long as he was needed back in London for an urgent meeting with Prime Minister Tony Blair.

But once he arrived, he was literally bowled over by what he saw, he ripped up his prepared speech and spoke from the heart and at some length, shouting at one stage to his aide, who was at the back of the marquee manically waving his arms to tell him he had to leave, 'Tony can wait!'

It all worked out well in the end. The client was delighted and their profile increased massively as a result too, which of course had a positive effect on their property sales' values.

And the coverage

Here is an extract from one of the many articles from the event, published the following week in *The Sunday Telegraph* by Sonia Purnell, one of the national journalists who attended, which sums up its success. The coverage went on and on, and Newhall's profile, and the values of property at the development, continued to shoot up as a result.

> 'When John Prescott pulled up in one of his famous black Jaguars for a tour of the new village of Newhall on the outskirts of Harlow last week, few expected what was to come...
>
> "I'm getting excited down here," he explained animatedly, "I didn't have one before but I've got a vision of the future now. I've seen it. So often it's missing, but you've got it here. You've got the wow factor. I want planners to beat their way here. I want the principles behind this to be what all new developments are about."'

Back at work in the office with Nikki, my hours, in the early days, fitted perfectly into my home life. I just worked a few days a week, always leaving in time to collect the children from school, and not the school holidays. It worked well, and came to an end only when she took her business to London to blend it with a big property marketing company. I had to factor in

travelling to and from London which didn't work for me and the family, so we parted company amicably.

PUBLIC RELATIONS LESSON

For your PR to work you need to understand that it is *not* all about you or your business. It is about really getting to know, and working closely with, those people who will give you that valuable third-party endorsement to your target audience. The better they know and like you, the more they will rave about you, and your target audience will listen and take heed.

Tactics to help make this happen for you include:

1. Find out what they are really interested in, or are fans of, and try and link it with things that you have in common with them.

2. Always be consistent and keep in touch regularly. Whoever your influencers are, you need to be making sure that you are at the front of their mind. For example, email and phone target journalists regularly to find out what they are writing about and how you might be able to help.

For an event to be a success from a PR point of view, it needs careful planning and close attention to detail. Here are four things to remember:

1 Create a spreadsheet for everyone involved, covering all the details, including every eventuality and every photographic opportunity.

2 Brainstorm, think out of the box and write down everything that you may or may not need. Allocate each item as the responsibility of a particular member of the team.

3 Be as flexible as you can with your plans, and constantly update the spread sheet as things change.

4 Offer your journalists a range of angles for your event so that you can get as many different media covering it for you as possible.

CHAPTER EIGHT

Going It Alone

> *PR is extremely important, and being able to use it in the right way means everything. You have to market your success.'*
>
> *Lee Haney, bodybuilder and former Mr Olympia*

Over the next few years I ran my consultancy, on my own, based at home with mainly property clients, sometimes using a freelance copy writer to prepare my press releases, but mainly doing everything myself. And juggling it around the childrens' routines.

During this time, I realised how important it is to be constantly keeping up with what is happening in the news, having my antennae up for any angles in my clients' target media that they could comment on or add to. I had all the national and local papers and magazines that had property supplements, delivered each week, and my husband brought back the *Evening Standard* from London every Wednesday as it has a big property section.

I studied them carefully, noted which journalists were writing what, and in the general news sections I monitored what was being written about in case I could weave my clients into any stories in any way.

As soon as I read something that I thought my clients could comment on, add further information to, or support with a case study, I would email or telephone the journalist and try and pitch them in. It worked many times and they used my ideas. At worst, they just thanked me for trying, and explained that the story was over and nothing more would be done. At least it gave me another reason to speak to them, which is always good.

I have also always listened to BBC Radio 4's *Today* programme from when it starts at 6.00am, even in Luxembourg, with the radio balanced precariously on the window ledge of our bedroom as it was the only place I could get a signal. The *Today* programme is widely held to be the place where any news of the day is first reported. Often by lunchtime that same news is being put out on different news channels, also on chat shows like *Jeremy Vine* on Radio 2, and the morning television programmes.

I rang the researchers on these radio and TV programmes several times over the years trying to work my clients into the relevant stories which I knew were being covered, and only narrowly missed out each time because my

clients were just not well known enough for the media to use them, or they had already gone to someone else in the industry.

But that should not stop you doing the same for yourself or your own business. One day they will be looking for exactly what you are offering and your tenacity will win you the coverage over your competitors.

I would make phone calls from the car, whilst walking the dog, waiting for the children to come out of school, or before meeting friends for coffee – and you can do the same.

Retirement – not mine

After a few years as Lucy Matthews PR, I was introduced to the owner of a property marketing company, Craven Property Services, which did all the design, artwork, print, and advertising for property developers, including the hoardings and sales cabin designs at their developments and even training for their sales teams on site. All they didn't have was property PR.

So in I went to run the PR arm of it, taking my existing clients with me. I had one girl working for me, the brilliantly conscientious and talented Michelle, and together we grew Craven's PR clients from two or three to about 14. They were very busy times but great fun and I learned loads again, that PR infiltrates everything you do if you want to build a business and make connections.

At Craven, I experienced first-hand the value of using my PR skills to boost my chances of getting new business: being friendly, complimentary and easy-to-get-along with, rather than pushy and selling myself.

At a new business pitch for a property developer client in Chichester, I set off with a strategy and it worked. Before the meeting started, I sat with the receptionist chatting animatedly about her job and thanking her for helping me park my car and getting me some water. I then complimented the potential client on their office – its convenient location, choice of pictures on the wall, comfortable chairs, and I made them laugh and feel comfortable with me about something that had happened to me earlier in the day, so the atmosphere was relaxed and happy.

In the middle of my 'why you should work with me' speech, I was interrupted by the Chairman, who turned to the MD of the company and said: 'I don't know about you, but I would pay that fee just to spend an hour a month with Lucy. It's obvious you are good at what you do, Lucy, but more importantly you brighten our day.'

I won the business, we got along brilliantly, and went on to do some great work together.

Another important client that we won in my early days with Craven was Churchill Retirement Living. A family-run business based in Ringwood, Dorset, building apartments

specifically for the retirement demographic, across the UK. We were taken on to do Churchill's entire national, local and corporate PR, and so began my love affair with the retirement property market, which is still going strong to this day.

I left Craven after a couple of years to return to working for myself (taking the clients I had brought in back out again) and Churchill Retirement Living eventually came and joined me, after the appropriate exit time from Craven; I worked for them for 10 years altogether. They are now such a big business they have employed in-house PRs so do not need a consultant role like mine anymore. So sad for me, as I loved my time with them.

PR strategies and timelines

Of the many things I learned from working with my property developer clients such as Churchill Retirement Living was the value of creating and implementing well-thought-out PR strategies and processes, set into a structured time-line, which were employed for each live site (developments in various stages of build and sales from pre-planning through to the finished all-sold-out product). These generated masses of coverage each month, really helping to lift their profiles and position them as leaders in their field alongside their major (and more established) competitors.

At any one time for Churchill we had at least 20 live sites, and each month we wrote a series of press releases covering one or more of the following subjects:

❯ Crisis management statements and comments for the local press of sites going through the planning stage, providing a balanced view to those of disgruntled locals and NIMBYs (Not In My Back Yard), who had gone to the press and were often ill-informed about what this new development was that was being planned for their town.

❯ Work just started on site.

❯ Case studies of happy customers.

❯ The launch of a new service in the developments such as on-site hairdressing.

❯ Anniversaries/milestones such as a resident's 100th birthday, or three years since the development was started, or the 25th development to be launched.

❯ Sponsorship of a local charity and any fund-raising events. For example, they were a big supporter of Macmillan nationally, so every development would have its World's Largest Coffee Morning for which we would do PR in the relevant local papers. And in the head office, the Chairman and MD would do some kind of publicity stunt each

year to get into their local and property trade press. One year they had their heads shaved and it was photographed and got loads of coverage, even making the news/gossip section of their leading trade publication, which was very good for their corporate profile.

❯ Naming competitions, which were a real success. Basically, we would prepare a press release asking local people to suggest a name for the development, offering a prize for the best name and reason behind it. The release explained the competition and the prize, and we pitched it to the best local paper in the area who ran it for free as editorial, the entries came in to the client who selected the best, I then interviewed the winner and prepared a second press release which was run with a picture of the winner with their prize outside the development (complete with branding) and the release ran in the same paper again. Two bites of the cherry and every-one was happy.

❯ Various events at the developments such as the official launch (for which Lionel Blair was our VIP), Christmas, Easter and Summer parties etc.

Churchill Retirement Living (CRL) asked us to prepare monthly coverage reports detailing how much coverage we had achieved and giving its value relative to an

advertising spend in that publication. Through these I had real proof of the value of PR – and the widely-held rule of thumb that each piece of coverage is worth 500 times that of an advertisement.

PR brings business

Back in the home office I became an official company, MPR Ltd, created at Companies House in August 2007. Working for myself again with my trusted copy-writer (also working from home, so we rarely met) I began to gather some good new clients, all coming to me through various forms of PR. I have never advertised my PR consultancy for retainer clients and have never been short of work.

Two estate agent clients asked me to work for them with no competitive pitches, thanks to a recommendation from one of my national journalist friends, Graham Norwood, and at the same time I acquired a second retirement developer, Renaissance Villages (RV), this time building retirement villages at the higher end of the price bracket from CRL, so a perfect fit for me.

The CEO of RV, Bill Gair, rang me and asked if I would like to work for his company, as he had met me at a few property events over the years, and had heard that I was doing a good job for an estate agent in Surrey who was selling his second hand properties (from purchasers who bought the new build property

when the retirement development had just been completed and were now moving on).

Proof in my own life, of the value and importance of networking and third-party endorsement from relevant influencers.

RV proved to be another fantastic client for us and we worked for them for over 10 years, ending only because they sold the brand to another developer.

I had always appreciated the value of forward features in trade and consumer publications and the importance of forging strong working relationships with relevant journalists so that they began to rely on me for good stories (from my early days with Minden Luby). Now I really got to grips with these two PR fundamentals working in the national media.

Through my PR strategies with RV and CRL I made it my challenge to find out when every retirement feature was running in the national newspapers and relevant consumer magazines, and who was writing the stories, to ensure that my clients were included in them. We achieved 100% success. We only missed out on those where they were either focussing on areas of the country in which my clients were not building, or on a different sector of the retirement market. Three interesting things happened as a result.

Become the go-to source for journalists

Firstly, I became known among the regular journalists who worked on these retirement property features as the go-to PR for relevant good 'oldies' stories, and they would sometimes come to me with ideas for a story first to see if I could help make it substantial enough to pitch to the editor of the section.

Secondly, I started to get my other journalist contacts into the ever-growing retirement property editorial market, suggesting story ideas they could pitch to the editors, and therefore getting a double whammy – a commission (and fee) for my journalist contacts and good coverage for my client, plus profile building for me.

Thirdly, I collaborated with fellow PRs, who had complementary retirement developer clients, although not in direct competition, so that we could provide the journalists with a totally oven ready story.

For example, when we knew what stories the features were running, and the angles they were looking at, we would contact each other and work out which of our clients had the best case studies or examples of the angle, and present them to the journalists as a package. The results were better all round for everyone – our clients got excellent coverage, the journalists didn't have to work as hard, and we were all helping each other. Those were good times.

We were so successful that PRs with clients in direct competition with mine would ring me up mock-complaining that they were fed-up with seeing my 'same old photos in every supplement!'

There was the 80-year-old who lived in an RV retirement village who did a sky dive for charity; the retired publican who had previously cared for his wife with Alzheimer's and had no life until she went into a home and he moved into the village and made new friends, continuing to visit his wife every day, and running the bar in the village as a volunteer in the evenings; and the couple who met and married in a CRL development.

And with all the economic and social implications as our population is living longer, there was never a shortage of news angles and stories for us to write press releases about and pitch national story ideas.

I learned a lot about the value of PR and what we could do through working with Bill Gair for over 10 years on his developments, and watching how he used it to his benefit.

He had been in the house building industry for around 30 years. During that time, he created and sold two companies and he is convinced that the reason he achieved such good ultimate sale prices for the businesses was due to the strength of his own profile – he is widely

held to be 'the doyen of the retirement development world' – and because of the high perceived value of his products.

And that has all been achieved through his long-term concentration on PR, and the sheer number of column inches and interviews, both press and radio, he has achieved through years of PR campaigns in the relevant media.

Bill was always very active in the property industry and keen to raise his profile ahead of his competitors, especially in the very competitive retirement housing market. As a past President of the House Builders Federation, a director and Chairman of NHBC Building Control, and a member of numerous committees and organisations, he lobbied the government on various issues, and was sure that it had been due to the PR he used, that his messages got out there, and his expertise was recognised.

As a direct result, potential buyers approached him, twice, with bids to take over his businesses and he was able to dispose of them off market and at acceptable prices.

His raised profile – having his name, and that of his company mentioned in all the relevant media – also meant that his business was always expanding as good land-buying opportunities kept being brought to him

(before his competitors), joint venture partners were always wanting to work with him, and he never had a problem raising investment for his projects.

Bill's long-term use of PR also helped increase his revenues through being able to maintain good sales prices for his properties.

I learned in meetings that he always kept a very close eye on where his enquiries and sales come from, with copious reports drilling down to every detail of a customer's journey, and he was confident that his PR campaigns were a major contribution to his businesses' continuing sales success. They were able to maintain their prices through very tough times and never had to resort to price reductions.

Being mentioned in every retirement feature in *The Daily Telegraph*, *The Times*, *The Sunday Times*, *Saga* and other press outlets that his demographic read and trusted proved to work.

He used to say that in his many years of business he came across plenty of non-believers and cynics who either focused on other forms of marketing, or stopped using PR during the tough economic times. But he never did. PR remained an important tool to him, despite having to curtail other activities, and he said that its relatively lower fees proved a very good return on investment.

He never stopped investing in PR, which meant he was able to maintain vital momentum in the media, with journalists coming to him for comments and putting his stories, comments and properties into articles ahead of his competitors because he was always there, with a steady flow of material given to them every month. This is what ultimately made the difference in the success of his companies compared to some of his competitors.

Regular media presence meant that the potential buyers of his properties, and his businesses, knew he was a constant in the industry, a brand they could trust whose longevity was proven by the years (and reams) of media coverage they found every time they opened the property sections or googled him.

This is what people do now to check a company's viability. And if there are no mentions of the company or the individual in the media that potential buyers know and trust, they will not be impressed.

Working with Bill and Renaissance Villages was eye-opening as there was so much we could do, and they were very open to new strategies and trying out PR ideas.

Awards, alliances, events and community sponsorships

I began writing a lot of award entries then, and still do today, mainly for the property awards, of which there are many. Being short-listed, and winning them, is a major boost to an organisation's profile, credibility, and ability to charge more for its properties and services, attract better calibre staff and win land and investor deals.

We arranged a lot of events in the various retirement villages we were promoting to bring in potential buyers, including a May Day Fair complete with stilt walkers, an old-fashioned trio of musicians, and maypole dancing; a typical English village fete with stalls such as a coconut shy and fortune teller and a falconry display; and a weekend of events in the new clubhouse demonstrating all the activities which could be enjoyed if one moved into the village. These included ballroom dancing, swimming, gym workouts, cocktails, afternoon tea with a string trio and evening drinks parties on the terrace entertained by a close-up magician. All the events brought in loads of new visitors, engendered great community spirit and so increased sales.

We liaised with local organisations and set up sponsorships for the developer, including Liphook in Bloom, and the local open gardens events, which raised money for the

village church fund. Again, this created lots of good local community feeling for the retirement village, which was becoming a major part of the existing village life.

Alliances are always a good idea for bringing different groups of customers together, and we arranged and publicised a few for RV, including a local household name making good quality furniture and whose target audience was very similar to RV's. We did a joint promotion, featuring their furniture in the show homes, and they promoted the village in their shops. It was very successful.

PUBLIC RELATIONS LESSON

You need to be interesting and newsworthy for your target media to use you, and your stories should be something that their readers (your target audience) would want to read about.

Here are some angles you can use, in any business, to make you appealing enough for your target media to write about you:

1. Anniversaries, new business, new staff members and hosting an event.

2. Sponsorships, charity work, and alliances.

3. Case studies, trends and survey results.

4. Competitions and awards.

5. News from your industry, national days.

CHAPTER NINE

The Marvellous Entrepreneur PR Paradox

> 'If I was down to the last dollar of my marketing budget I'd spend it on PR!'
>
> Bill Gates

I hope you have gathered by now that PR is an incredibly powerful tool, as Bill Gates acknowledges. Everyone should be using it to grow and strengthen their businesses as well as to benefit their personal lives.

Yet I have found a tragic resistance to using it by the very people who really need it. A paradox that I have dedicated the rest of my career to trying to change.

In January 2012, I decided I needed to grow my business and make it more sustainable, as I wanted a better work/life balance and to plan an exit strategy for myself for when I was ready to stop trading my time for money.

Up until now, this is exactly what I had been doing for my clients, with only my copywriter preparing press

releases for me. Essentially, I was only being paid for the hours I was working myself, so there was only ever a finite number of clients I could work for at a time, and I had no space for my own personal growth.

I recognised this, but was not entirely sure how I was going to change things at that time. Then I started to do a lot more networking and discovered the marvellous world of the entrepreneur.

Entrepreneurs Circle

I joined the Entrepreneurs Circle, a national organisation created by the serial entrepreneur Nigel Botterill, providing marketing advice, support and encouragement to small business owners and entrepreneurs across the UK. By throwing myself into every meeting, event and opportunity that came my way during the three years that I was a member of the organisation, everything changed for me. I learned so much about myself, what I could do with my business, and the pains and dilemmas of my fellow small business owners.

Every month I attended really buzzing meetings in various parts of Surrey, led by the inspiring and seriously funny marketing whizz, Vanessa, as well as the big one-day national events held around the country with motivating guest speakers, lots of marketing, business and self-development learnings and masses of networking

opportunities and mutual support from fellow small business owners. It was so much fun and things started happening fast for me.

It only took two months for me to spot the perfect niche for myself in this world, which led to masses of new opportunities and another new path opening in front of me.

PR for entrepreneurs

I recognised that despite talking about the 12 marketing pillars that everyone should have in their business to be successful, sell more, and make more money, the Entrepreneurs Circle was only paying lip-service to PR. They had no one on their staff with any PR experience to help members understand and use it fully.

And these people, my fellow members, were just the type of business owners who needed PR most. As their businesses were mainly small, their potential customers did not know about them as they were bad at shouting about their successes. And the owners all wanted to lift their profile in their market sector, and they all had limited budgets.

However, their perception of PR was that it is only for the big boys and a luxury they could not afford, so they did not spend time finding out what it was

all about and what they could be doing, at no extra cost, themselves.

The PR paradox was there, right in front of me, and I realised I had to find a way of helping them – and that would be my niche. I wanted it to be my personal mission to help small business owners shine a light on how marvellous they are, without boasting.

I named myself the UK Entrepreneur's PR Expert and, as far as I could see, this was something that traditional PR agencies had never done before. Which made it even more exciting for me.

Invest in your most important asset – yourself

The result, several years on, is a whole new side to my world and my business. My success can be measured by my results. To date I have reached over 10,500 people since I started my How To Do It Yourself PR resources and I am inspiring more each day to just get on and do PR.

I now have A Marvellous Reputation, financial freedom, an excitement every day about getting to work, and a fantastic work-life balance with a clear goal for the future of my business, and myself alongside it.

I had already started on the road of self-development, reading a few books and attending a weekly Practical

Philosophy class, which taught me the importance of mindfulness, and how to practise it.

Now I went up a gear. I spent much more time and money really investing in myself, and growing the Do-PR-Yourself side of the business. And I have not stopped since.

My thirst for knowledge and love of learning, together with my lucky ability to grasp things quickly, has made it a brilliantly enjoyable journey, and I know there is so much more ahead for me.

I am never too tired or too busy to take on another learning opportunity. The children laugh at how much time and money I spend on courses, books and conferences, but I love them and everything I have learned has been put to good use. A big lesson is that it is really important for your business, and personal success, to invest in your most valuable asset – yourself.

Develop yourself, review and reflect, educate, invest in, and improve yourself.

Why not invest in PR?

This has led me to constantly question why more people do not therefore invest some of their time each month in learning about, and doing, PR for themselves and their businesses. It can cost them nothing if they do it

themselves, and the returns can be immense. Surely it is an investment of time worth doing?

I read Michael Gerber's brilliant book *The E Myth*, the premise of which struck a massive chord with me as to why I had no exit plan, and what I needed to do to create one.

The essence of the book is that as business owners we all have three elements to our personality – the Technician, Entrepreneur and Manager. We need all three to make our business a success, but we also all tend to be more of one element than another.

Michael Gerber argues that the reason most businesses fail is that they are run by the Technician who is too involved in the job and there is not enough input from the other two personality traits.

He says that the Technician is the person who actually does the job that the business is selling, i.e. bakes the cakes, mends the bicycles, programmes the computers, does all the PR for clients, etc. These people decide to set up their own business because they are good at their particular craft and want to take 100% of the profits for themselves, not giving them to someone else that they are working with. They tend to be thinking only about the present and not doing all the other things needed for a successful business. And this is where the problems lie.

The Entrepreneur has the vision, wants to get on and do something novel and looks to the future, thinking about what the business can achieve and where it could go.

And the Manager is the more pedantic details person, who is well organised, predictable and a safe pair of hands, sorting out paying the bills and keeping everything in order.

Gerber says we all need these three components to run a successful business: the vision of the Entrepreneur provides the Technician with much more than just doing the job he was previously doing for someone else. And without the Technician's expertise, the Entrepreneur would have to get someone else to do the work. And if there were no Manager, the business would not run at all.

Work *on* the business

The big idea that hit me from the book was the need to work *on* the business rather than *in* it. I needed to create systems and bring in other people who could run the business without me having to do everything, so that I could lift myself out from being the technician and the business could eventually run without me.

I could then achieve the financial freedom and work/life balance I was after. And it has worked.

From those early days, I read and learned about:

- ❯ Neuro Linguistic Programming (NLP)
- ❯ Transactional Analysis (TA)
- ❯ Myers Briggs Type Indicator (MBTI personality programming)

and how to use them in my personal and business worlds.

I also started reading or listening to loads more inspiring self-development books. Audible has been the best piece of technology for me, and I listen to masses of books now while I am driving, doing the housework, doing the gardening, or on walks.

So many important things have struck me from them. I started keeping these inspiring ideas like mantras in my mind, often referring to them, and as a result I have been able to grow both personally and commercially more than I would ever have imagined. I keep updating my mantras after I finish each new book.

This personal growth and change of mindset gave me the confidence and inspiration to set big goals. I looked outside my world as a consultant, being paid only for the hours I worked, stepped way out of my comfort zone, and created something new, something I could be proud of, possibly eventually sell or pass on to someone else to run, and which would carry on paying me when I decided to stop working.

Some of my mantras

Here are some of the mantras which are most important and useful to me:

❯ Asking myself each day, what is the one thing I need to do today that will make my boat go faster?

(See *Will it make the boat go faster?* by Ben Hunt-Davis MBE)

❯ Asking myself several times a day when I feel I don't know what to do next, what is the one thing that, if I was to do it now, would make everything else I want to do easier for me?

(See *The One Thing* by Gary Keller and Jay Papasan)

❯ Who you hang around with matters. Which means we need to be around other positive energy givers – not emotional drains.

(See *Botty's Rules* by Nigel Botterill)

❯ Become a marketer not a doer – we need to spend as much time *on* the business as we do *in* it.

(See *E Myth* and *Botty's Rules*)

❯ Invest in myself and constantly keep learning so that I am being the best I can possibly be.

(See *Botty's Rules*)

❯ Do the task I am most dreading first, and everything else will then seem easier.

(See *Eat That Frog* by Brian Tracy)

Albert Einstein said:

> 'The definition of madness is doing the same thing
> every day and expecting a different result.'

❯ Recognise and change some of the habits that are holding me back from success.

❯ Failure is OK. We are judged not by what we do wrong, but by how we pick ourselves up from problems and carry on.

❯ JFDI – Just f*****g do it. If you don't try, you won't ever know if it would have worked.

❯ Life is not a rehearsal.

❯ Champions are not born. They spend hours and hours practising and perfecting their craft. So I must do the same with everything I turn my hand to.

(See *Bounce* by Matthew Syed)

❯ Spend money on experiences with others rather than things – they will make you happier.

(See *The Happiness Advantage* by Shawn Achor)

I have many more. These are just the important ones for now.

21 Days to form a habit

'Outcome is not in your control. What is in your control is your effort and your intentions.'

Amit Sood

My self-development learnings suggested I needed to get some good routines going in my life, and research shows that it takes 21 days for something to become a habit. Many of the books I read around the habits of successful people pointed to them having strict routines in their lives to which they stuck rigidly, and which helped put them ahead of their competitors.

I decided I wanted to do the same and instate some new habits into my life, giving them all 21 days to get set into my routines so that I stuck to them, and so that it felt wrong not to be doing them.

Four years on, I truly believe these habits contribute to the success I am enjoying today – and the rosy future I can see ahead of me.

My new habits include:

❯ Setting my alarm for 05.45am each morning, listening to *Farming Today* on Radio 4 (I know, but it really is so interesting) while I adjust to waking up, and at three minutes to 6am when they tell me about the weather for the day,

getting up, making a hot drink and sitting down at the computer for an hour and a half to work on my business. No distractions, emails and phone off, house all quiet, and focussing only on stuff that will grow the business and bring in more paying clients.

❯ Setting goals and creating a vision board each year, which is stuck on the wall next to my desk for inspiration. On every January 1st I get my goals from the year before and review them, writing out what I want to achieve this year, and what it will feel like, looking back in a year's time. I then précis the notes into a short-list that I store in my phone case so I can refer to it often.

❯ Doing an hour's Body Balance and meditation twice a week – a combination of yoga, Tai Chi and Pilates.

❯ Eating healthily and practicing mindfulness regularly.

❯ Having tennis lessons at least twice a week, to re-learn how to play doubles, and then practising as often as I can.

❯ Listening to books and podcasts on long journeys, walks, or doing chores, to expand my mind and learn more.

❯ Learning how to do all the things I need in my business before delegating them to others, like

the book keeping, social media and ad campaigns, technology, website stuff, Facebook and LinkedIn ads, email marketing etc.

❯ Regularly investing some of the profits from the business on courses and mentoring for my own self-development.

❯ Committing to a mastermind group and spending a day per month with its members; and setting up groups of small business owners local to me for mutual support, sharing the highs and lows and learning together.

❯ Giving regular time each month to a local charity as a trustee.

❯ Saying yes to every opportunity to learn something new and putting 100% energy into it.

❯ Investing a lot of money in, and committing many hours each month to, a powerful CRM system, Infusionsoft, to build my database and provide free education-based campaigns to my 2,600 followers helping them develop an understanding of what PR is and encouragement to JDFI.

The birth of Marvellous PR

Through these new habits, I totally changed the way I did my business. I created a brand distinct from myself, called Marvellous PR, as it is a word I use a lot and starts with M, the first letter of my official Companies House name, MPR Ltd. The logo was designed with bubbles around it to reflect my bubbly personality apparently.

I transformed from a PR professional working one-on-one with clients, to a business owner in charge of others. I was no longer a doer – I was an entrepreneur. I burst from the confines of considering my business as an income and saw it as an entity in itself.

I brought in six freelance PR and social media consultants to do the day-to-day work for my clients, and I pulled myself away from that side of the business, keeping a close eye on my retainer clients, being involved in strategy and ideas generation, but spending more time helping small business owners and entrepreneurs learn how to get PR going in their businesses themselves.

I have always been a bit different from my peers, and I think it gave me a little more strength of purpose when I realised I was on a less-trodden path with whatever I was doing. I am experiencing that again now.

What now makes me different from any other PR company I have come across are my DIY products designed to empower businesses and take the fluff out of everyone's

perception of PR. And the structure I set up of strict goal setting achieving each milestone, and doing lots of networking and PR for the business continues to elevate Marvellous PR and these products and resources, to even greater success every month.

Productisation

Within the PR consultancy sector, developing products to enable businesses to do their own PR was, and still is, very rare. To potentially cannibalise sales from retained clients with a product, which gives clients the tools to undertake PR activity themselves, would seem suicidal to the rest of the PR fraternity. My PR peers aired their fears of this happening when we met for a Christmas get-together in the early years of my move into productisation.

However, I stuck with my mantras, kept looking forward with confidence, and thought, 'What did Sir Richard Branson do when people said he couldn't create a new airline, train service, bank, etc?'

Then I just got on and did it without much outside help.

In 2013, as The UK Entrepreneur's PR Expert, I launched my first course on how to do your own PR, called *Your Marvellous PR Toolkit*. Everything you need to know about why PR is such a valuable marketing tool, and all the information you need to get on and do it yourself.

I had professional videos and audios made of myself presenting and reading the material so that people who bought the course could choose to read it, listen to it in the car, or watch the videos. Or do all three of course. I had come full circle and was now really using my drama training, and passion for presenting, performing and selling on stage. A career I am now ready to do full-time.

I have discovered that, as I had initially thought, giving businesses the tools does not eat into my potential customer base; it expands it. As a result, I have become synonymous with PR amongst the broad range of businesses and individuals whom I have reached through my expanding range of products.

Giving out the help and offering support while they learn how to do it, has positioned me as a trusted authority, the go-to expert on PR for growing businesses. My transformation from business owner and practitioner of my profession to entrepreneur is the result of a change in my mindset. Without this change, I wouldn't have considered creating a product. I would not have sold my toolkits and resources and I would not have been able to help so many SMEs demonstrate how fantastic they are to their customers. Without them having to boast.

My plan to put my business on autopilot will continue. I have become an expert marketer and teacher, providing

loads of free help and information each week to thousands of small business owners and entrepreneurs. I have proved that offering a huge amount of value really is good for business (and makes you feel great, too).

My original PR Toolkit has now totally sold out and I have a new updated version – Lucy Matthews' Publicity for Profits Formula™. This, A Marvellous Reputation and my other PR resources have become my tools through which I engage entrepreneurs and small business owners that never considered PR as a viable means of marketing their business.

Alongside this, I have launched numerous automated marketing campaigns after rolling out Infusionsoft. As well as nurturing prospects and making the business stickier, my regular twice-weekly education-based emails make a serious difference to over 2600 business owners every week (at the time of writing).

I have received masses of positive feedback from recipients who act on my emails and are now doing more PR as a result.

For example, Stuart Barrow who runs Promoting Independence wrote to me recently saying that he had been receiving his regular messages and that day they pushed him into action. He had been listening to BBC Wales, which was talking about housing benefit, and he decided to call in with some advice. The presenter

asked if he would be interested in being contacted in the future which he agreed to. He had never thought he would do anything like that before, but, he said, I had encouraged and pushed him.

I am helping others do the same. I have understood the importance of the process as much as the end goal. Along the way, I have helped develop young people who were keen to forge a career in the world of PR with a tailored work experience programme. Designed to give them a hands-on, practical grounding on PR within the marketing mix, the programme is helping produce the next generation of PR consultants. To date, 10 young people have worked with me, resulting in five of them going on to work in either PR consultancies or marketing/ PR roles.

I now have several books, DVDs, workbooks, templates, on and offline toolkits and packages that business owners can buy which teach, help and support them in getting PR working for their business and embedding the habit into their working routines. (See www.lucymatthews.co.uk for more details).

Implementing the PR habit

My driving passion about PR and business then, as now, is that if I could get new habits going in my life which were proving phenomenally successful, so could others by spending time each week on their PR.

You don't get anything from doing nothing – but you can get huge results from doing something positive and strategic in your business every day/week/month/year.

One of the lovely entrepreneurs I have helped is Jane Maudsley, founder of the Little Voices franchise. She bought my *Your Marvellous PR Toolkit* in a franchise version to use to build the corporate business profile, and for each franchisee to build their own profile in their local area. She is brilliant, has implemented everything I suggested and has had great success since taking my advice.

Demystify and make PR simple

A huge part of my entrepreneurial mission, since 2012, has been to demystify PR, how it works and the process of securing press coverage. I have aimed to change the perception of PR amongst business owners who considered it fluffy, irrelevant to their business and a luxury only big companies and celebrities could afford.

I became the resident PR expert for the Entrepreneur's Circle, developing the workbook on PR for all the local monthly meetings across the country; providing one-to-one half-hour consultations at Millionaire Master Plan Four-Day events; and presenting on stage to 150+ members at one of the national events.

I began creating and delivering numerous seminars and workshops; speaking at events; creating my own and sharing webinars with other marketers; appearing on other marketers' podcasts; and undertaking massive social media engagement through blogging, Twitter, Facebook and LinkedIn. The impact of this on my SME and entrepreneur followers has been incredible.

Individually, business owners tell me that they have gained hugely from the PR they have been doing. Media exposure has not only generated buzz around their business, it has given them a chance to shine. And the more they shine, and tell others who inspired them, the more their third party endorsement of me has helped build my business.

Parent-teacher-meeting-PR

One of the best exercises I did for Entrepreneurs Circle, and which I would love to create again myself as it was so valuable to the businesses I met, was at the three Millionaire Master Plan events.

About 150 members at each event spent Saturday and Sunday immersed in learning all the elements they needed to turn their businesses into million-pound successes, from managing their numbers, to raising their personal profiles, to deciding which marketing tools would work best for them.

Then on the following Monday and Tuesday they had access to a room full of experts with whom they could spend 30 minutes at a time, for free, to help them implement what they had learned. I was the PR Expert.

It felt rather like a parent-teacher meeting, with tables set up round the room labelled with our name and what we did, and the members had to fill in a form on the Sunday evening requesting who they would like to talk to. We were then given lists of these people whose appointments started at 08.30am and carried on, with no breaks, until 6pm.

I remember the trepidation of going up to my allotted table on the first morning of the first of these events, seriously thinking that it would be really embarrassing as no-one would want to chat with me. Most people in Entrepreneurs Circle really didn't understand what PR was, and how valuable it could be for them, so why would they want to talk to me, I thought? I would be sitting there all day like Nobby No-Mates sipping my tea and doodling on my notepad.

How wrong I was.

Both my days were jam-packed with people wanting my advice and by the end of the second I was exhausted and hoarse from all my conversations, but energised like I had not been for many years in my job – and totally

buzzing from the light bulb that had gone off in my head. This was my new niche.

Simple plan: market, media, message

It was so fun and interesting. We had 30 minutes for me to find out exactly what the business owner did (or was aiming to do, as many of them were coming up with new ideas for businesses), who they wanted to attract and therefore which media would be the best route for them.

Right up my street – using my natural curiosity and eagerness to please. Then I helped them craft their basic messages and came up with as many ideas as I could for how they could make themselves interesting to those journalists, in order to get their messages across.

A very basic Market, Message, Media exercise that every business owner needs to do when planning their PR strategies.

PUBLIC RELATIONS LESSON

Small business owners and entrepreneurs need PR the most as they need to cut through the noise and get their messages heard, and be seen as the go-to expert they know they are in their world. PR is the most cost-effective route for them and everyone should be setting aside some time each week to do PR for themselves and their businesses.

Five tactics to remember in terms of getting PR into your life:

1 As Michael Gerber suggests, put equal emphasis on all three elements of your personality – the Technician, Entrepreneur and Manager, and work on the business not in it.

2 Have mantras you can repeat that help you have confidence to stick to your plans and strategies.

3 Set up some new good habits to make sure you are doing PR regularly and properly.

4 Create and stick to a simple plan focussing on your market, media, and message. Work out who you want to attract, which media would be the best route to get you in front of them and which messages would work most strongly.

5 Work on your own self-development that will then reflect on the success of your business as those you come into contact with, will naturally tell others how marvellous you are.

CHAPTER TEN

Telling The World

> 'If you talked to people the way
> advertising talked to people
> they'd punch you in the face.'
>
> *Hugh MacLeod*

Throughout this book, I have touched on how I have seen the use of PR skills work brilliantly in my personal life as well as helping clients and fellow small business owners make more money in their commercial worlds.

I want to expand now on how it has worked for me, in my personal life – and how it could be of use to you.

Settling into communities

During my adult life, as you can see, I have moved from London to Australia, Surrey to Luxembourg, Guildford to Totnes in Devon, and at each stage I needed to make friends for myself and the family, settle us into the community and expand my work in one way or another.

I have done it successfully through using my basic PR skills, that work just as well in a business networking event, or a new client meeting, or schmoozing with journalists, as they do when you are trying to establish yourself in a new community – or just want to make new friends where you have lived for years.

I have learned that it is really important to listen more than to speak. As they say: 'God gave us two ears and one mouth and we should use them in those proportions.' When I meet people I ask them lots of questions about themselves, getting them to talk about their lives, families, work, hobbies and interests, that immediately makes them feel comfortable with me, that I am interested in them, and often makes them like me.

I always make eye contact with people I have just met, give them my full attention when we are talking and try and find something to complement them on too, which, again, makes them like me. When other people join us to chat, if the new person has not met the person I am talking to I always introduce them, highlighting the positive things they have just told me about themselves, and thereby making myself even more valuable to them.

Well, I have not had anyone tell me I have been annoying with these tactics, so I hope it has been good for them too! I have certainly met lots of new people who have become close friends over the years using skills like these.

Third-party endorsement for achieving goals

Let's look at being a little more strategic and how you can use the hugely powerful third-party endorsement element of PR to achieve your personal goals whilst remaining authentic to yourself of course.

You need to work out who would be the most valuable influencer of the person, or group of people you are trying to attract, meet them, and get them to introduce you to the group or individual you are targeting.

For example, say you have decided you would like to join a book group, you have listened to what people are saying about the different groups in your area and decided the one that seems like it would suit you best, is run by someone you do not personally know. How do you get an introduction, and get accepted into the group?

You need to find someone you know, who is well known and liked in that group and whose opinion will therefore be listened to by the organiser. Meet up with them, give them all the ammunition they will need to persuade the person who runs the group that you would be an asset to it, and then ask them if they would be so kind as to have a word for you and just gauge the possibility of your joining. You would be: 'so grateful for your help, and do ask if I can do anything for you in return?'

The reason for giving them the ammunition is just the same as working with journalists. It is making your acquaintance's life easier for them – so they don't need to work out for themselves why you would be a good fit for the group. You have already told them.

Your acquaintance then, armed with the positive reasons why you would be good for the book group, only has to make one phone call and repeat what you have told them, and the job should be done.

Here is another example that I helped with recently.

My friend is a tennis coach and wants to expand his horizons to a nearby club where he is not known. We worked out together who he knew at this new club, and there were a couple of people. So, we made ourselves think as strategically as we could, looking at which of these people had the most influence in the club and focussed our efforts on him.

I then helped my friend list all his own positive qualities and experience: who he had coached previously; their successes; what people had said about working with him and how nice he was etc; and how well he had done himself in his own tennis career. Then my friend took this virtual list (in his head) and met up with his acquaintance in the new tennis club. He is now running coaching sessions there too and they all really like him.

Another mantra to remember in these situations, where you are basically selling yourself into a new group or to a new friend, is that you must totally avoid being an advertisement for yourself.

Does PR work?

Yes, yes, yes!

Through every stage of my career I have seen proof of its power, value and amazing return on a relatively small investment.

The general perception about PR is it's all fluff and its results aren't quantifiable. My clients would disagree.

I have always worked closely with every client to ensure they enjoyed significant return on their investment, whether measured by profile building, sales growth, cost-savings or productive time clawed back.

Matthew Byatt from my client Newhall, summed it up:

> 'The results of Lucy's PR work, whilst sometimes difficult to quantify, are evident by the hundreds of column inches of coverage achieved by her – space which, if bought, would cost hundreds of thousands of pounds. In a world of multi-million-pound marketing budgets spent promoting a product or service by increasingly odd methods, there is one sure-fire way of getting the message across – PR.'

I help my clients become savvy in online and traditional media, enabling them to smartly identify and capitalise on publicity opportunities. For many, I am integral to their marketing team.

I developed a version of my *Your Marvellous PR Toolkit* to work for franchises, to help them build their profile by teaching the franchisees how to exploit local media and gain free publicity – as well as the franchisor how to work on their corporate profile. One of my first buyers of the Franchise toolkit, who concentrated hard on building the profile of their brand, recently sold the business for £25m.

Every single resource I have launched has been designed to show business owners how to become magnetic to publicity and the value they will gain from it.

It is so exciting to know that I have personally empowered thousands of business owners to take control of their public image and dip their toes into PR for the first time, marketing their business more effectively and better spotting opportunities for publicity.

All change

My business and I have changed completely now, transforming from a PR professional - exchanging fees for hours worked - to an entrepreneur running a PR agency with four options – we do it all for you, you work with our property team, you learn to do it yourself, or you use us only when you need us. And this now provides me with multiple income streams.

Most importantly, I've demonstrated that, by giving incredible value and sharing knowledge and experience willingly, you can make a significant impact on the fortunes of fellow business owners, which is something I am so proud of.

In my personal life, by recognising and honing the amazing power of third-party endorsement, networking skills, NLP, body language and communication tactics such as maintaining eye contact, asking lots of questions and mirroring my companion's movements, I have quickly created fantastic social networks for myself and my family, everywhere we have lived. These have been so strong that they have lasted years after we have moved on from a particular place.

I now live in Totnes, in the glorious South Hams region of Devon, UK. It is a beautiful market town at the head of the estuary of the River Dart, complete with a castle built in AD 907 and some wonderful buildings from

the 16th and 17th centuries. It has a reputation for being very hippy and New Age and is a thriving centre for music, art, theatre and natural health. People laughingly say it is twinned with Narnia. I love living here and the bohemian madness of the town gives me just the right balance from my busy PR world to make my life a real delight.

My world of PR as a career, and Marvellous PR, has allowed me to move to Totnes from the commuter world of Guildford in Surrey, to work the hours I want whilst making the most of the countryside, the sea and the wonderful people and activities on offer here. It has also given me goals which, once I have achieved them in a year or two, will enable me to travel extensively, play more tennis, learn new hobbies and skills and spend more time with my wonderful family and friends.

I do hope you will be inspired to use the full extent of PR in your personal and work life. It is one of the most valuable things you can do for yourself and your business - finding the right people to tell the world, or at least those people that matter most to your business and your personal life, how marvellous you are, without you having to boast.

Thank you for sharing my world and good luck with yours.

PUBLIC RELATIONS LESSON

PR skills can work just as well in your personal life as in your business world. Approaching all your relationships with a PR mindset can help you to establish yourself in a new community or refresh your friendship group.

Here are five tactics for making PR work for your personal life:

1   Remember to ask lots of questions and listen more than you talk. Always give more than you take.

2   Maintain eye contact, study body language, give your full attention and try to find something to compliment them on.

3   Work out who the influencers are of your new group – and help them to be your third-party endorsement, for you.

4   Avoid being an advertisement of yourself. It is all about them, not you.

5   Networking is brilliant PR for you and your business, as long as you use it strategically and stick to the tactics outlined above.

10 Public Relations Lessons For Entrepreneurs Who Want To Be Talked About

Here is a summary of the lessons I have discovered and shared with you throughout *A Marvellous Reputation*. I hope they prove as valuable to you as they have always been to me – and remain so today.

1

As PR is all about **communicating effectively** with the people who influence your target audience, there are vital skills you should know and use all the time. Dale Carnegie summarises the most important fundamental techniques for successfully handling people. See Chapter One.

2

The real strength of PR lies in the fact that there is no hard sell. It is all about the value of **third-party endorsement** – so it is vital that you find, get to know, and regularly communicate your messages to those influential people who will then tell your target audience how marvellous you are, without you having to boast. See Chapter Two.

3

Case studies are the fundamentals of third-party endorsement and it is therefore important for your PR that you are collecting, writing and pitching them to your target media on a regular basis. Dig deep and ask lots of questions when you are collecting your information as there may be a more interesting story in the case study than just that they have used your product or service successfully. See Chapter Three.

4

Every business should have a crisis management plan in case the worst happens to it, and working with journalists and building strong, respectful relationships with them are fundamental for good PR. See Chapter Four.

5

Implementing a **well-thought-out PR and Marketing Strategy** will make a real impact on your business and its bottom line, if undertaken consistently and with laser focus on who your target audience is and who their influencers are. See Chapter Five.

6

For your PR to work well, you need to be **following a formula,** which can be used in any industry – and in our personal lives: finding the angle that will interest the journalists (or other influencers), preparing a good pitch to sell it to them, and developing really good relationships with your target media (or influencers) so they trust you. See Chapter Six.

7

Planning everything, including every eventuality, every photographic opportunity and creating, updating and sticking to very comprehensive, and flexible lists is vital for the PR success of **an event** you are arranging. See Chapter Seven.

8

You need to be **interesting and newsworthy** for your target media to use you, and your stories need to be something that *their* readers (your target audience) would want to read about. See Chapter Eight.

9

For your PR to be a success, you need to create, and stick to, a simple plan focussing on **Market, Media, Message.** Work out whom you want to attract, which media would be the best route to get you in front of them and which messages would work most strongly. See Chapter Nine.

10

PR skills can work just as well in your personal life as in your business world. **Approaching all your relationships with a PR mindset** can help you to establish yourself in a new community or refresh your friendship group. See Chapter Ten.

I would love to help you make PR work in your business and personal lives so that you can have lots of the *right* people talking about *you* – and raising your profile.

There are several ways I can do this – either by showing you how you can do it yourself, or by arranging for it all to be done for you by myself and my colleagues.

Please go to my website at www.lucymatthews.co.uk and then get in touch with me via email at lucy@lucymatthews.co.uk

FURTHER READING

The following books have been hugely influential for me. I am grateful that their authors wrote them and I was able to use them for my own advantage:

Book Title	Author	Publisher/Year
Be a Purple Banana	Jez Rose	Dr Zeus Publishing (March 2015)
The Millionaire Clown	James Sinclair	Meroe Books (Feb 2015)
How to Win Friends and Influence People	Dale Carnegie	Vermilion (April 2006)
Do it or Ditch It	Bev James	Virgin Books (July 2011)
The E Myth Revisited	Michael Gerber	Harper Business (March 2001)
The Chimp Paradox	Prof Steve Peters	Vermilion (January 2012)
Will it Make the Boat Go Faster	Harrier Beveridge and Ben Hunt-Davis	Matador (June 2011)
Key Person of Influence	Daniel Priestley	Rethink Press (September 2014)
Oversubscribed	Daniel Priestley	Capstone (April 2015)
The Happiness Advantage	Shawn Achor	Virgin Books (Sept 2011)
Black Box Thinking	Matthew Syed	John Murray (April 2016)
Cognitive Behavioural		The Great Courses (June 2015)
Leap First	Seth Godin	Sounds True (Feb 2015)
The Big Leap	Gay Hendricks	HarperOne (May 2010)
Speak So Your Audience Will Listen	Robin Kermode	Pendle Publishing (Oct 2013)

Life in Half a Second	Matthew Michalewicz	Bolinda Publishing (Aug 2014)
Pitch Anything	Oren Klaff	McGraw-Hill (Feb 2011)
Crush It	Gary Vaymerchuk	Harper Business (Sept 2013)
Becoming Steve Jobs	Brent Schlender and Rick Tezeli	Spectre (Mar 2016)
The One Thing	Gary Keller and Jay Papasan	Bard Press (April 2013)
The Four-hour Work Week	Timothy Ferriss	Vermillion (Jan 2011)
Purple Cow	Seth Godin	Penguin (Jan 2005)
Thinking Fast And Slow	Daniel Kahneman	Penguin (May 2012)
Talk Like Ted	Carmine Gallo	Pan (June 2017)
Profit First	Mike Michalowicz	Portfolio (Feb 2017)
The Pumpkin Plan	Mike Michalowicz	Portfolio (July 2012)
The Seven Habits of Highly Effective People	Stephen R Covey	Siimon and Schuster (Jan 2004)
Screw It Let's Do It	Sir Richard Branson	Virgin Books (March 2006)
The Willpower Instinct	Kelly McGonigal	Avery Publishing Group (Dec 2013)
Eat That Frog	Brian Tracy	Hodder Paperbacks (Jan 2013)
The Slight Edge	Jeff Olson	Green Leaf Book Group (Nov 2013)
Bounce	Matthew Syed	Fourth Estate (April 2011)
Open	André Agassi	HarperCollins (Aug 2010)
Botty's Rules	Nigel Botterill	Vermillion (Aug 2011)

ACKNOWLEDGEMENTS

I thank everyone who has inspired me, given me confidence to get on and write this book, and supported all my ups and downs in confidence. In particular, my family: Paul, Hannah, Jess, George, Simon M, Simon L, Nicky, Adam, Sarah, Charlie T, James, Henry, Bryoney, Kyle, Nick, Al, Saira, Barcley and Charlie S-J; my mastermind group; Dave, Keith, John, Jo and Pete; my fellow PR colleagues Bea, Katy, Katie, Sarah, Lucy, Bracken, Alex, Ellie, Amanda, and Henrietta; my fellow entrepreneurs, inspirers and graphic designers; Mark C, Thom, Vanessa, Martin N, Barry, Vicky, Veronica, Emma S, Stu, Laura M, Iain P, Daniel P, Ben H-D, Helen D, Julia, Neil, Kate, Mike, John, Nicci, Carie, David H, Ashley, Rich, Mark W and Francis; all my wonderful supportive friends whom I am scared to list in case I miss someone out; all the many authors whose books have been so inspirational to me: James Sinclair, Dale Carnegie, Jez Rose, Bev James, Michael Gerber, Prof Steve Peters, Harrier Beveridge and Ben Hunt-Davis, Daniel Priestley, Shawn Achor, Matthew Syed, Seth Godin, Gay Hendricks, Robin Kermode, Matthew Michalewicz, Oren Klaff, Gary Vaymerchuk, Brent Schlender and Rick Tezeli, Gary Keller and Jay Papasan, Timothy Ferriss, Daniel Kahnerman, Carmine Gallo, Mike Michalowicz, Stephen R Covey, Sir Richard Branson, Kelly McGonigal, Brian Tracy, Jeff Olson, Matthew Syed, André Agassi, and Nigel Botterill; Charlie Mullins for writing the foreword and Lucy and Joe and their team at Rethink Press for their amazing help getting the book out into the world.

THE AUTHOR

Lucy Matthews is a highly driven, successful entrepreneur and businesswoman, PR expert and performer with over 30 years' experience in the world of PR. She has helped thousands of entrepreneurs and small business owners to understand and use the power and value of implementing PR in their work and personal lives. She is widely regarded as the UK entrepreneur's PR expert.

Lucy has worked with a huge range of clients in B2B and B2C markets, around the world, from industrial floor cleaning manufacturers, to football clubs; property developers to therapists; Pepsi to pasta ready meals; photographers to authors; big businesses to entrepreneurs and small start-ups; helping them all to build their profile, make more sales and put themselves ahead of their competitors.

Her career has taken her in and out of consultancies, big and small, and finally into running her own busy PR consultancy, Marvellous PR, and creating her bespoke courses and materials, Lucy Matthews' Publicity for Profits Formula™, handy reference guides and PR

Planners, all with the aim of providing everything small business owners and start-ups need in order to do their own PR, with back up help from her consultancy if they need it.

This book is her answer to all the PR cynics and non-believers, taking you on her journey to realising the true power and value that good third-party endorsement can bring to our lives, and giving you 10 Public Relations lessons/tactics you can use now to make your business, and your life, super successful.

For help going forwards please visit her website:

🏠 www.lucymatthews.co.uk

🅕 www.facebook.com/MarvellousPR

🅧 @MarvellousPR

🅛 www.linkedin.com/in/lucymatthewspr

RETHINK PRESS

First published in Great Britain 2017
by Rethink Press (www.rethinkpress.com)

To the Me
Fe

A *Marvellous*
REPUTATION

10 LESSONS FROM MY LIFE AS
A PR INSIDER FOR ENTREPRENEURS
WHO WANT TO BE TALKED ABOUT

All The best,
Lucy

LUCY MATTHEWS